Usborne Art Ideas
Drawing
Cartoons

INTERNET-LINKED

Anna Milbourne

Designed by Jan McCafferty and Catherine-Anne MacKinnon

Illustrated by Jan McCafferty, Gary Dunn, Christyan Fox, John Richardson, Paddy Mounter, Catherine-Anne MacKinnon, Sarah McIntyre, Uwe Mayer, Neil Scott, Andy Hammond, David Pattison, Adam Stower, Antonia Miller and Ian McNee

Additional illustrations by Alex de Wolf, Anna Milbourne, Kevin Faerber, Geo Parker, Stephen Cartwright, Vici Leyhane and Ainsley Knox

Additional design by Andrea Slane, Antonia Miller and Vici Leyhane

Cover design by Mary Cartwright

Photography by Howard Allman

Americanization by Carrie Seay

Internet links

Throughout this book we have recommended websites where you can find lots of ideas to help you draw cartoons. To visit the sites, go to the **Usborne Quicklinks Website** where you will find links to all the sites, plus pictures from this book that you can download and use in your own projects.

1. Go to **www.usborne-quicklinks.com**
2. Type the keywords for this book: **drawing cartoons**
3. Type the page number of the link you want to visit.
4. Click on the links to go to the recommended sites.

Here are some of the things you can do on the websites recommended in this book:
- Take cartoon drawing lessons with famous cartoonists.
- Make your own comic strips online.
- Watch a video clip lesson on how to draw a cartoon superhero or a princess.
- Find out how animated films are made and create an animation online.
- Learn how to draw lots of different cartoon characters and watch cartoon clips.

Site availability

The links in Usborne Quicklinks are regularly reviewed and updated, but occasionally you may get a message that a site is unavailable. This might be temporary, so try again later, or even the next day. Websites do occasionally close down and when this happens, we will replace them with new links in Usborne Quicklinks. Sometimes we add extra links too, if we think they are useful. So when you visit Usborne Quicklinks, the links may be slightly different from those described in your book.

Downloadable pictures

Pictures marked with a ★ in this book can be downloaded from the Usborne Quicklinks Website. These pictures are for personal use only and must not be used for commercial purposes.

A COMPUTER IS NOT ESSENTIAL
TO USE THIS BOOK
This guide to drawing cartoons is a
complete, self-contained book on its own.

Safety on the Internet

Ask your parent's or guardian's permission before you connect to the Internet and make sure you follow these simple rules:
- Never give out information about yourself, such as your real name, address, phone number or the name of your school.
- If a site asks you to log in or register by typing your name or email address, ask permission from an adult first.

What you need

To visit the websites you need a computer with an Internet connection and a web browser (the software that lets you look at information on the Internet). Some sites need extra programs (plug-ins) to play sound or show videos or animations.

If you go to a site and do not have the necessary plug-in, a message will come up on the screen. There is usually a link to click on to download the plug-in. For more information about plug-ins, go to Usborne Quicklinks and click on "Net Help".

Note for parents and guardians

The websites described in this book are regularly reviewed, but the content of a website may change at any time and Usborne Publishing is not responsible for the content on any website other than its own.

We recommend that children are supervised while on the Internet, that they do not use Internet chat rooms, and that you use Internet filtering software to block unsuitable material. Please ensure that your children read and follow the safety guidelines printed above. For more information, see the Net Help area on the Usborne Quicklinks Website.

Contents

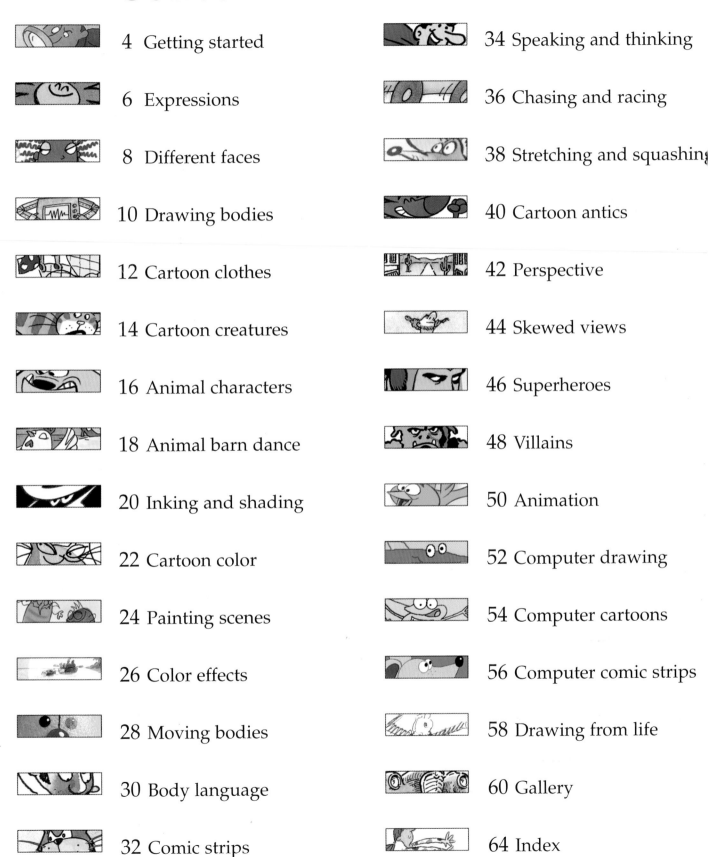

Getting started

All you need to start drawing cartoons is a pencil and some paper. Look at cartoons on television, in comics and books, or on the Internet for inspiration. Here are some ideas of more things you can do to get started.

Drawing and collecting

Cartoonists keep sketchbooks which they fill with lots of drawings, ideas and information. Keep a folder and fill it with sketches of cartoon ideas, postcards, comics and strips from newspapers.

Sketch people in different positions for future reference.

Keep a sketchbook of your cartoon ideas.

Buy comics for inspiration.

KISS ME QUICK

I'M CUTE

HIYA BABE

Collect comic
strips printed in
newspapers.

Collect postcards
of famous cartoon
characters.

WALT DISNEY'S
MICKEY MOUSE
©Disney

Ideas

As well as using pencil to
draw cartoons, this book
explains how to use other
materials, too. It also contains
lots of ideas for drawing
different styles of cartoons.

Find out how to draw characters
showing emotions on pages 30-31.

Find out how to make moving
cartoons on page 50.

Find out how to draw
superheroes on page 46.

★ Look out for this star symbol
throughout the book. It marks pictures
which you can download from the
Usborne Quicklinks Website.

☞ For links to websites where you
can take cartoon drawing lessons
with famous cartoonists, find ideas
to get you sketching and read comic
strips and cartoons online, go to
www.usborne-quicklinks.com

Expressions

An essential part of drawing cartoons is being able to draw expressions. You can draw lots of different expressions very simply. Then, you can use these to create complete cartoon characters.

☞ For links to websites where you can find lessons and tips on how to draw cartoon faces and expressions, and watch a video demonstration, go to **www.usborne-quicklinks.com**

A basic face

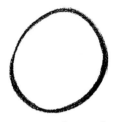

1. Draw a rough oval shape. It needn't be too neat. If it's lopsided it will add character.

2. Draw two small ovals for eyes, and put dots in them. Add a curve for a mouth.

Changing expressions

Using just the eyes and mouth on a face, you can draw all sorts of expressions. Copy the faces on the fruit below and try combining different eyes and mouths to vary their expressions.

Grinning

Surprised

Bashful

Sleepy

Sad

Laughing

Mischievous

Angry

See page 59 for more expressions.

6

Making a character

A basic circle face, with just a mouth and eyes, already has lots of personality. Without adding much more, you can make simple cartoon characters. For example, just add legs to make a spider, or add wings and legs to make a flying insect.

Find out more about how to show movement on pages 36-37.

In a cartoon garden, even the flowers can have faces.

Different faces

A simple circle can make a person's face, but it's fun to vary the shape of faces you draw to give your cartoons different characters, like the ones you can see here. Experiment with drawing different hair, eyes, noses and mouths.

Grinning girl

The ears are level with the nose.

1. Draw a circle for the head. Add little curves for the eyes and nose. Add a semicircle for a mouth.

2. Draw a line across the mouth. Add vertical lines for the teeth. Add ears halfway down each side.

3. Draw lines for pigtails on both sides of the head. Draw a few lines for bangs. Add dots for freckles over the nose. ★

Worried man

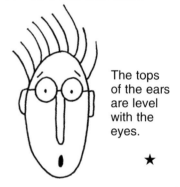

The tops of the ears are level with the eyes. ★

1. Draw a long oval for the head. Add circles with dots in them for eyes. Between the eyes, add a very long nose.

2. Add an oval mouth. Draw a line to join the circles around the eyes. Add lines to the sides of the head for glasses.

3. Draw two curves for ears. Add little lines for raised eyebrows. Add long lines for hair on top of the head.

All of these faces were drawn using black felt-tip pen. Then, some parts were added or filled in using colored felt-tip pens.

Angry bad guy

1. Draw the head as a curved shape with a flat bottom. Add a line for the eyebrows. Then, add a rectangular nose.

Add little lines inside the ears.

2. Draw curves from the nose to the eyebrows, and add dots in them for eyes. Draw ears, level with the eyes.

Add a line above the eyebrows.

3. Draw a big downward curve for a mouth. Add a smaller one beneath it. Add dots on the chin for stubble. Draw lines for hair.

Cool lady

1. Draw an oval face. Add oval eyes, with a line across each one. Then, add pupils looking to one side.

2. Add a small nose. Draw an 'm'-shape and then underline it for the top lip. Add a curve for the bottom lip.

3. For the hair, draw a big curve from the top of the head. Join it to the face at the bottom. Do the same for the other side.

To create this crowd scene, the people at the front were drawn first, then the people farther back.

As well as varying the people's faces, try varying the shapes of their bodies, and their clothes.

Drawing bodies

In cartoons a character's body can be whatever shape you want it to be. Here are some tips for drawing cartoon people's bodies. You can vary the shapes to get different characters.

In the comic *Asterix*, the two main characters are completely different sizes.

©2002 LES ÉDITIONS ALBERT RENÉ/GOSCINNY-UDERZO

☞ For links to websites where you can learn how to draw famous cartoon characters and find more drawing tips, go to www.usborne-quicklinks.com

Body proportions

Cartoonists can vary the body proportions of their characters to create different effects. For example, the bigger the head looks in proportion to the body, the cuter or more child-like the character will look.

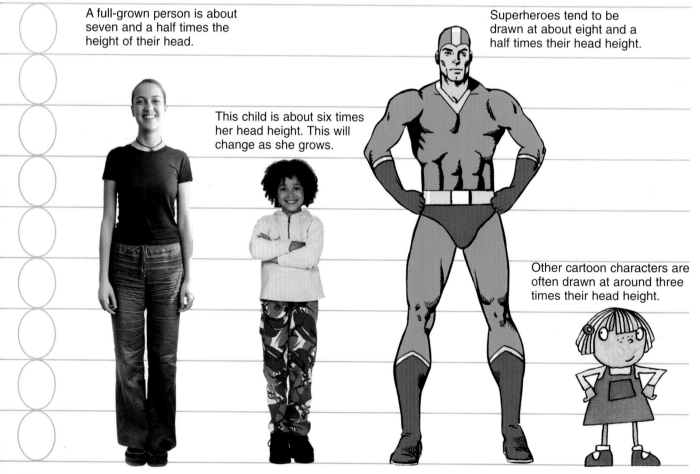

A full-grown person is about seven and a half times the height of their head.

This child is about six times her head height. This will change as she grows.

Superheroes tend to be drawn at about eight and a half times their head height.

Other cartoon characters are often drawn at around three times their head height.

Body building

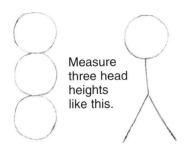

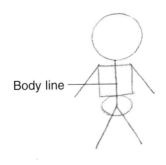

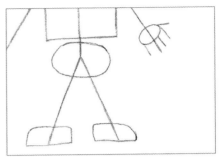

1. In pencil, draw a circle for the head and then a line for the body. Add two stick legs coming from the body.

2. Add a rectangle for the ribs and an oval for the hips. The legs start halfway through the hip oval. Add stick arms.

3. For the hands, draw ovals and add stick fingers and thumbs. Then, add feet to the bottoms of the stick legs.

4. Draw a face and hair using techniques and ideas given on pages 8 and 9. Add two lines for the neck.

5. Draw a T-shirt and pants. (See page 12 for more about clothing.) Then, outline the arms and the hands.

6. Go over the outline using a felt-tip pen. Leave it to dry, and then erase all the pencil lines inside the figure.

Use the step-by-step instructions above, but vary how big you draw each part to get different body shapes.

This robot is short and squat. Try drawing a tall, gangly one too.

To draw an older child, make the arms and legs longer.

A gorilla has very long arms and short legs.

11

Cartoon clothes

Adding certain types of clothes to a cartoon character can help show who the character is. For instance, a cowboy hat, jeans, a neckerchief, and boots are often used to show a cowboy; a tall, puffy hat and white clothes are often used for a chef.

Chefs can have checkered pants, too.

Clowns usually have face paint and a red nose. They can also wear very big shoes.

This is Desperate Dan from the comic, *The Dandy*. He is a larger-than-life cowboy who always dresses in these clothes.

Cartoon burglars usually wear a striped top and an eye mask.

Superhero family photo

Draw the faces next to each other.

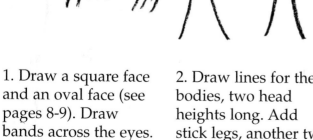
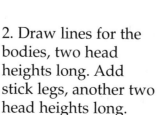
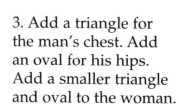
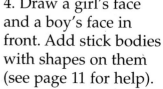
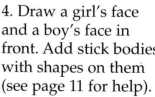

1. Draw a square face and an oval face (see pages 8-9). Draw bands across the eyes. Add the hair.

2. Draw lines for the bodies, two head heights long. Add stick legs, another two head heights long.

3. Add a triangle for the man's chest. Add an oval for his hips. Add a smaller triangle and oval to the woman.

4. Draw a girl's face and a boy's face in front. Add stick bodies with shapes on them (see page 11 for help).

12

5. For the outline, first draw the neck. Then, draw the arms as far as the wrists. Add the body up to the waist.

6. Next, draw the outline for the legs. Add oval feet on the ends. Then, draw hands on the hips.

7. Draw the cloak, adding 'v' shapes around the neck. Add lines for the edges of the boots and gloves.

8. Draw over your outline using felt-tip pen. Erase all the pencil lines. You can then color it in.

To draw more serious superheroes, use the proportions suggested on page 10, and follow the steps on page 46.

This picture was drawn using permanent felt-tip pen, and painted using watercolors (see pages 22-23).

Cartoon creatures

Animals are lots of different shapes and sizes. However, you can use the same, simple shapes to draw all kinds of four-legged animals. All you have to do is vary the sizes of each part of the body.

Use these basic shapes to draw all kinds of four-legged creatures. You will need to add different snouts and tails for different animals.

Make the neck and legs a lot longer for a giraffe.

Shorten the legs and neck, and move the head down for a tortoise.

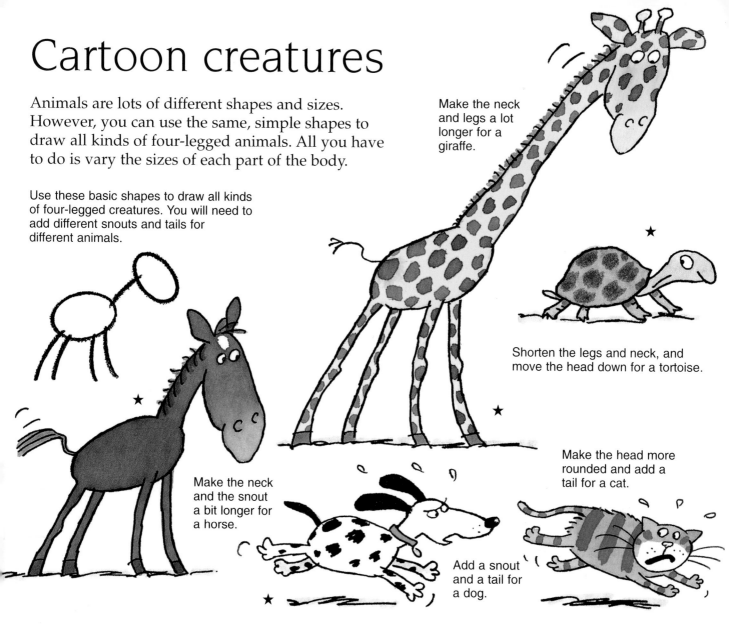

Make the head more rounded and add a tail for a cat.

Make the neck and the snout a bit longer for a horse.

Add a snout and a tail for a dog.

People and their pets

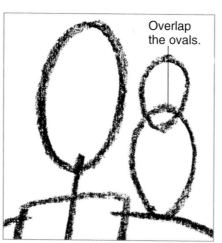

Overlap the ovals.

1. In pencil, draw shapes for a man's body using the steps on page 11. Don't add the face yet.

2. On the man's shoulder, draw an oval parrot's body with a head on top. The ovals should overlap a little.

3. Draw a big, curved beak on the parrot's face. Draw a big, beak-like nose on the man's face. Add the man's mouth.

4. Add big, oval eyes on the man's face and on the parrot's. Add the pupils, leaving a little white dot in each for highlights.

5. Draw the parrot's feathers and the man's hair. Add the parrot's toes. Draw the man's suit. Add his hands and shoes.

6. Outline the two bodies in felt-tip pen. Let them dry, and then erase the pencil lines. Then, you can color them in.

Use the basic shapes for animals from page 14 and people from page 11 to draw more people and their pets. Make them look similar by drawing similar faces or hair. Here are some examples.

This scene was drawn in permanent felt-tip pen and painted using watercolors (see pages 22-23).

This woman's hair makes her look like her poodle. Her sweater looks like its fur, too.

This girl has a long face like her horse. Her hair looks like the horse's mane.

This man has fuzzy hair like his dog's ears. Their coats are similar too!

15

Animal characters

You can give different animals of one kind, for example cats or dogs, personalities of their own. Vary their expressions and body shapes to create different characters.

In the cartoon *Duckula*, each character is a different kind of bird: the nurse is an enormous hen, the butler is a vulture and Count Duckula, of course, is a duck.

☞ For links to websites where you can learn how to draw famous animal characters including *Scooby Doo*, and find tips on drawing cartoon animals, go to **www.usborne-quicklinks.com**

©FremantleMedia Enterprises Ltd.

Butch bulldog

1. Draw a circle for the face. Draw a line for the eyebrows and then add eyes. Add a nose, a mouth and pointed teeth.

2. Add curves from the mouth for jowls. Add the body. Then, add stick legs with oval paws, ears and a tail.

3. Outline the legs, tail and ears. Add a patch on its back. Add lines for the wagging tail and draw lines on the paws.

Snooty pooch

1. Draw a bean-shaped head. Add eyes, a nose and a mouth. Draw a cloud shape for fur, and a line and fur for an ear.

2. Draw a long bean shape for the body and add a cloud shape at the bottom. Add stick legs with paws, and a stick tail.

3. Add more cloud shapes for fur around the neck, on the legs and on the end of the tail. Fill in the paws and the nose.

Scruffy mongrel

Add little lines by the tail.

1. Draw an oval for the head. Add an oval snout. Add lines and ovals for ears on top. Add the nose and a tongue.

2. Draw a body. Add stick legs and a curved stick tail. Then, draw shaggy fur on the ears and over the eyes.

3. Add more shaggy fur on the rest of the body and the tail. Add some fur to the snout. Fill in the nose.

Draw the dogs in pencil, then use felt-tip pens to outline them and fill them in.

17

Animal barn dance

Another way of drawing cartoon animals is to stand them up, give them clothes and make them more like people. You can draw the animals in human situations to add to the humor.

Dippy giraffe girl

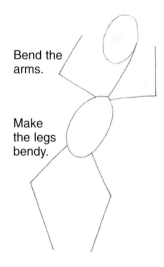

Bend the arms.

Make the legs bendy.

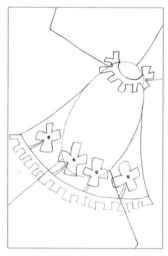

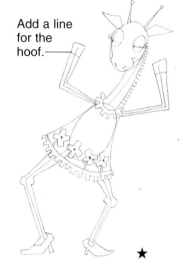

Add a line for the hoof.

1. In pencil, draw an oval head. Add a long stick neck. Draw a slanted oval body. Then, add long stick arms and legs.

2. Draw horns and ears on the head. Add eyes with lines for eyelids and lashes. Then, add the snout, mouth and nostrils.

3. For the dress, draw a curved neckline and then add the sides and bottom. Add frills along the edges. Draw a pattern on the dress.

4. Outline the long arms, legs and neck. Draw lines along the neck for a mane. Add high-heeled shoes to the feet.

Honky-tonk horse

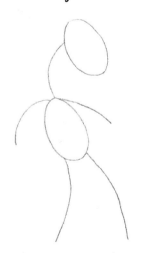

Make the neck quite thick.

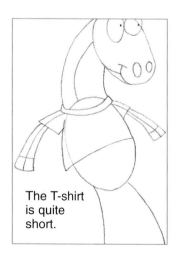

The T-shirt is quite short.

1. Draw an oval head. Add a curved stick neck and a long, oval body. Draw bendy stick legs and bendy arms.

2. Draw the ears and add the mouth. Draw oval eyes and nostrils. Then, outline the curved neck.

3. Draw a curved neckline. Add the rest of the T-shirt. Then, outline the bendy arms and add hooves.

4. Draw the waistband of the jeans and add a belt. Draw the rest of the jeans. Add pockets and a zipper.

These animals were outlined in permanent felt-tip pen, and then painted using watercolors. (See pages 22-23 for how to do this.)

A slogan was added to the horse's T-shirt.

I ♥ HAY

Dashes show the stitching on the jeans.

These hens have aprons on and are using their feathered wings as hands.

Spur

5. Add some cowboy boots. Draw heels and spurs on them. Then, add lines for the mane and tail.

You can make animals' paws into three-fingered hands, like this rabbit's.

19

Inking and shading

Most cartoonists draw cartoons in pencil first. Then, when they are sure the cartoon is correct, they outline it and fill in the dark areas with black. This is called inking. Here are some ideas for inking cartoons to get different effects.

Many comic strips that appear in newspapers, such as this *Garfield* strip by Jim Davis, are printed only in black and white.

Light and dark

You can bring cartoons to life and make them look solid by inking them to show light and dark areas. When light shines on something, the parts closest to the light are the palest and the parts farthest from the light are the darkest.

The light on this teapot is shining from this side.

Cartoonists often simplify shading into light and dark without using any medium shades.

Cartoons often use a window-shaped highlight on shiny surfaces, even if there isn't a window in the scene.

1. Draw the outline of the teapot above in pencil. Look at which parts are darkest. Outline them in pencil.

2. Go over the outline in pen. Then, fill in the darkest areas in pen. Let it dry, and then erase all the pencil lines.

3. The teapot is very shiny, so look at where the light hits it. Draw a little curved window shape there for a highlight.

20

Shadows

The size and shape of a shadow depends on where the light is coming from. A shadow always falls in the opposite direction from the source of light.

☞ For links to websites where you can watch video clips on how to draw *Garfield* and find more shading techniques, go to **www.usborne-quicklinks.com**

★

In the morning, when the sun is low in the sky, people throw long shadows along the ground.

In the middle of the day, the sun is directly overhead, so people throw short shadows.

At the end of the day, the sun sinks again. People throw shadows in the opposite direction from in the morning.

Dramatic lighting

You can use dramatic lighting to give a scene atmosphere. You can also use light and dark areas to make the reader look at a particular area of the cartoon. Here are some examples.

The two faces in this cartoon stand out because they are much lighter than the rest of the scene.

Silhouettes against a bright background can be used to show an evening scene.

A big shadow, like the one below, can look threatening or funny.

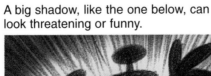

A shadowy face in a cartoon can look mysterious or threatening.

Cartoon color

Many cartoons have bright, bold colors. You can achieve these using felt-tip pens. However, many cartoonists use watercolor paints to add color and shading. Here are some tips on using watercolors.

Pen outline

To create a watercolor cartoon with a black outline, you need to use a permanent black felt-tip (one that doesn't blur when it gets wet). Before painting, draw the outline in permanent pen, then erase any pencil lines.

Using your pencil line as a guide, draw the outline in permanent pen. Let it dry, then erase the pencil.

If you only have a water-soluble felt-tip pen (one that blurs when it gets wet), then paint the cartoon first, and add the outline when the paint is dry.

Watercolor paints

Watercolor paints come in tubes, or blocks called pans. To use pans, rub a wet paintbrush on the pan to get paint on the bristles. Then, dab the paint onto a saucer.

Watercolor pan

Watercolor tube paint

To use tubes, squeeze a little blob of paint onto a saucer. Dab a little water onto it with a paintbrush and mix it in.

Add more water to get a paler color. For white areas, just leave a gap so the paper shows.

Leave a color to dry before painting another near it if you don't want them to blur.

Paint the lightest parts first and then the darker parts.

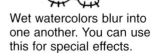

Wet watercolors blur into one another. You can use this for special effects.

Mixing colors

One advantage of using paint is that you can mix your own colors. There are three colors from which all other colors are made – red, yellow and blue. These are called the primary colors.

Mix yellow and blue to make green. Add more yellow or more blue to make different shades.

Mix red and yellow to make orange. Add more red or more yellow to make different shades.

Mix blue and red to make purple. Add more blue or more red to make different shades.

Mix red, yellow and blue together to make brown. To make different shades, alter how much you use of each color.

To make a color darker, add blue or brown. Try to avoid adding black, as it makes colors duller.

Green can be made darker by adding more blue. It can be made lighter by adding yellow.

25

Painting scenes

There are different ways of painting backgrounds using watercolors. These pages show two ways of painting backgrounds, and also watercolor techniques you can use to make a funny cartoon monster scene.

Painting backgrounds

1. Draw the whole cartoon, including the background, in permanent pen.

2. Paint clean water over the background. This will help you to get an even color.

3. On the damp paper, paint the background. Paint pale colors before the darker ones.

4. When the background is completely dry, fill in the foreground, or the main characters.

Monster moon scene

1. Dampen your paper by painting water onto it or by wiping a damp sponge on it.

2. While it is still damp, mix lots of a very pale color. Paint it on with a large brush.

3. While the paper is damp, mix a slightly darker shade and paint it on. The colors will blur together.

4. When the background is dry, mix a bright color and paint a blob. It doesn't matter what shape it is.

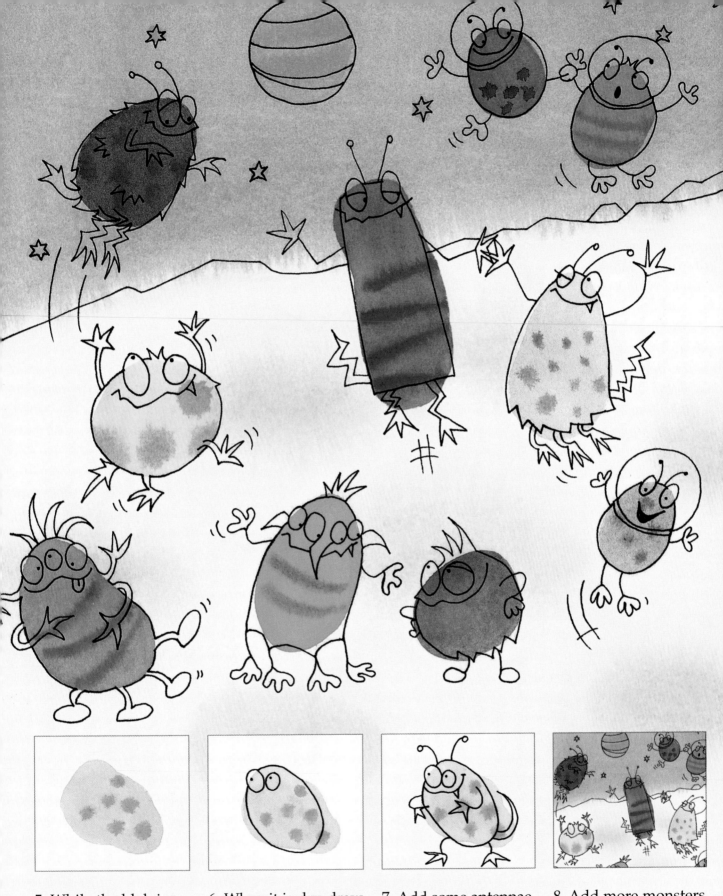

5. While the blob is damp, add little dots of another color. They will blur on the damp paper.

6. When it is dry, draw some eyes at the top. Add an outline. It doesn't have to follow the colored shape.

7. Add some antennae. Then draw some arms and legs. You can add a tail and other details, such as fangs.

8. Add more monsters to the scene following steps 4 to 7. Outline the planet and the rest of the background last.

Color effects

By using particular combinations of colors in a cartoon, you can create special effects. For example, you can use blues and greens ('cool' colors) to show a cold scene, and reds, oranges and yellows ('warm' colors) to show a hot scene.

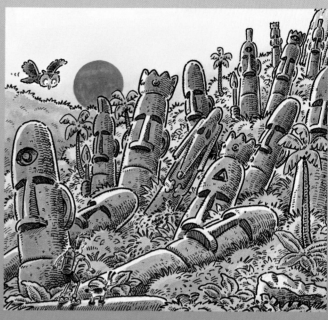

A rising sun might make the whole sky yellow and throw warm-looking light across a scene.

A snowy scene can be shown by using white with icy blue shadows.

A night scene can be shown using blue with yellow highlights.

In the spotlight

  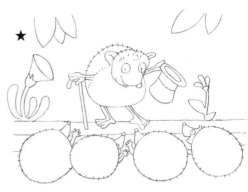

1. Draw a shape for the body. Add a head. Draw eyes, a mouth, ears and a nose. Then, add stick arms and legs.

2. Draw a top hat and a cane at the ends of the stick arms. Then, draw the arms and legs. Add the bristles.

3. Draw some more hedgehogs as an audience. Then, add a wall. Draw some plants and leaves around it.

4. Draw the outline in permanent pen and erase the pencil lines. Then, paint the yellow areas shown here.

5. Let it dry. Paint the blue areas. Then, mix shades of brown (see page 23) and paint the hedgehogs and the wall.

6. When it is dry, paint the plants in different shades of green and blue. Paint the hat and cane red.

Moving bodies

To draw a cartoon character from different angles you have to make it look three-dimensional. To do this, you can draw construction lines in pencil to help you get everything in the right place. You can erase these when the drawing is finished.

☞ For links to websites with tips for drawing cartoon characters from different angles, and examples of cartoon hands, feet and body poses for you to copy, go to **www.usborne-quicklinks.com**

Turning faces

Construction lines drawn on an orange can help you to see how the eyes, nose and mouth move when a face moves into different positions. The facial features always stay in the same position in relation to where the lines cross.

You can use these photos of a face on an orange as reference for how to draw a face in different positions.

Facing the front, the construction lines look straight.

Draw a circle. Add two construction lines making a cross inside. Then add the eyes, nose, mouth and ears.

Looking to the side, the vertical line looks curved.

Draw a circle. Add the construction lines, making the vertical line curve to one side. Then, add the face.

Looking down, the horizontal line looks curved.

Draw a circle. Add the construction lines, making the horizontal line bend downward. Then, add the face.

Looking upward, the horizontal line looks curved.

Draw a circle. Add the construction lines, making the horizontal line bend upward. Add the face.

Looking down and to the side, both lines look curved.

Draw a circle. Add the construction lines, making both the horizontal and the vertical lines bend. Then, add the face.

28

Turning bodies

To draw a body from different angles, you can use similar techniques to those used for the head. Here are some tips.

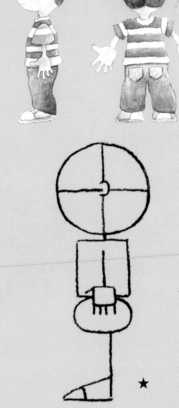

Use the shapes on page 11 to draw a body from the front. To draw shoes from the front, draw a triangle and then add a semicircle for the toe.

To draw someone turning slightly, draw a slanted square for the body. Add arms to the top corners. Draw triangle shapes for the feet.

From the side, one arm moves to the middle of the body shape, in line with the spine. The nearest leg completely overlaps the one farther away.

Focus on hands and feet

Cartoon hands and feet can have any number of fingers or toes. Many cartoon hands use only three fingers. You can adjust the following examples to fit any number of fingers or toes.

Hands

From the back, the body shapes look similar to those from the front. But only the backs of the ears show, and the feet are triangles without the toe shapes.

Feet

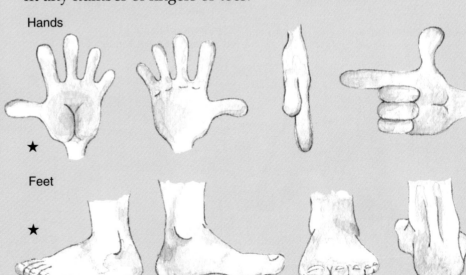

29

Body language

You can add comedy to cartoon characters by using body language to tell part of the story. This means drawing the characters in positions that show what they are feeling or doing. Cartoons tend to use very exaggerated poses.

©Disney

This man is reaching down with his arms and his legs are flying into the air with the effort of swatting at the fly.

In this picture, Donald Duck's fists are clenched and his brow is furrowed. His whole body position shows that he is furious.

A character might jump into another character's arms out of fright!

Someone reluctant to go somewhere might lean back.

Someone eager to go fast might lean foward as they run.

Someone waving their hands in the air and jumping can look overjoyed.

An unhappy character might look down and put their hands in their pockets.

A fatal attraction

Sometimes you can set a scene or tell a cartoon joke just using body language. The scenery can help add to the humor.

For links to websites where you can browse photo galleries of cartoon characters and study their poses, go to **www.usborne-quicklinks.com**

Add whiskers on each side.

Make the girl cat's eyes wide and add eyelashes. ★

Outline their heads before their bodies.

1. For a cat's face, draw an oval with a curve inside. Add eyes, a nose and a mouth. Add furry cheeks and ears.

2. Draw a girl cat's head, as shown here. Then, add oval bodies with stick legs and long tails. Add the feet.

3. Draw their clothes. Add shoes and other details. Then, outline them in permanent pen and rub out the pencil lines.

This scene was drawn in permanent felt-tip pen and then painted using watercolors.

The cats were drawn first and then the background was added.

A bird and some clouds were added here to show how high the drop off the cliff might be.

The worm looking over the edge shows how high the cliff is.

Comic strips

In comic strips, cartoonists draw boxes known as frames around each picture in the strip. Each frame shows a moment in time. Normally when you look at a comic strip you 'read' the frames from left to right, and from the top to the bottom of the page.

 For links to websites where you can create comic strips online and read lots of famous comic strips including *Peanuts* and *Garfield*, go to **www.usborne-quicklinks.com**

  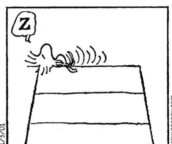

This *Peanuts* strip by Charles Schulz is a good example of a simple use of cartoon frames to tell a little story.

Framing the story

There are lots of ways that you can use frames in a comic strip. Here are some examples and tips on how to create a comic strip.

You can vary the size of the frames to make the strip more interesting or to make a point.

You can zoom all the way in to make an impact.

Make a character break out of the frame for a dramatic effect.

Before you start drawing the comic strip, make some rough sketches to work out how many frames you want to use.

Sometimes you can use just one frame to tell a joke or story.

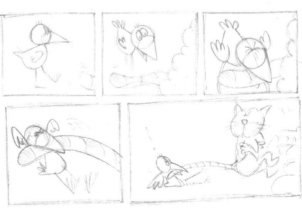

Sometimes a story is funnier if it's told using a few frames.

Mistaken identity

Before drawing the final comic strip, make sketches of the characters you want to use, to work out how they will look. To draw the comic strip below, first draw out the frames on the paper. Then, draw inside each frame using pencil.

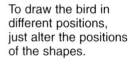

To draw the bird in different positions, just alter the positions of the shapes.

★

1. Draw a circle for a head. Add a triangular beak and a grin. Then, draw the eyes and tufts for feathers on the head.

2. Draw a semicircle for a body. Draw a wing and some tail feathers. Add stick legs and feet.

★

Add some whiskers, too.

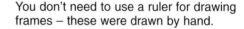

1. Draw a circle with a cross in it. Add the nose, then draw the eyebrows and eyes. Draw the snout. Add ears and fur.

2. Draw a big teardrop shape for the body. Add a long tail. Then, add stick legs and stick arms. Draw triangular paws.

3. Outline the arms – one overlapping the other. Outline the legs and feet, too, and add fingers to the paws.

★

This comic strip was drawn in permanent felt-tip pen and then painted using watercolors.

You don't need to use a ruler for drawing frames – these were drawn by hand.

Speaking and thinking

You can add words to single cartoons or comic strips, to make the characters speak, think or yelp, for example, or just to tell the reader what's going on.

For links to websites where you can find lots of ideas and tips on making cartoon lettering and visit a gallery packed with lettering styles (fonts), go to **www.usborne-quicklinks.com**

Speech bubbles

In comics, there are ways to draw speech bubbles so that the reader knows whether a character is actually talking, thinking, shouting or whispering. If you like, you can use pictures instead of words inside thought bubbles.

A cloud-shaped bubble like this contains thoughts or dreams.

This is a speech bubble. The tail should point toward the speaker.

The jagged edges on this speech bubble show that the character is shouting.

Drawing bubbles

When you add a speech bubble, draw it in pencil first, just in case your words don't fit and you need to make it bigger. When choosing where to position the bubbles in a strip, remember that you read comics from left to right and from top to bottom.

A speech bubble with dashes instead of edges contains a whisper.

1. Draw ovals for the speech bubbles using pencil. Then, add little, curved tails pointing toward each speaker.

2. Draw straight lines in the bubble and then write the text along them. Don't worry about fitting it all inside the bubble.

3. Go over the text in pen. If you need to, redraw the speech bubble so it fits around the words. Outline it in pen.

Speaking in character

You can use different styles of writing to show different characters' voices. Big letters show a loud voice and small letters show a quiet one.

Speechless

There are other ways of expressing a character's thoughts or reactions without using speech. Comics and cartoons use particular symbols to show certain things. Here are some examples.

A light bulb appearing over someone's head means they've had an idea.

An exclamation mark above someone's head shows their shock or surprise.

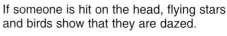

ZZZ shows that a character is asleep or snoring.

A question mark above a character's head shows their confusion.

Hearts can show someone's fallen in love. They can have hearts in their eyes, too.

If someone is hit on the head, flying stars and birds show that they are dazed.

Chasing and racing

There are tricks cartoonists use to show things moving in their drawings. Motion lines are the most common technique, but you can also add puffs of dust and words, or use a blurring effect to show movement.

☞ For links to websites where you can watch cartoon clips of the crazy vehicles in *Wacky Races*, meet the characters and find pictures and line drawings to inspire you, go to **www.usborne-quicklinks.com**

Zooming car

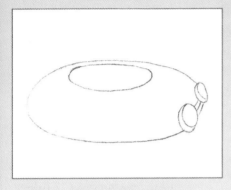

These are motion lines.

1. Draw an oval car body. Add another oval for the opening in the top. Draw headlights and a grill at the front.

2. Add slanted oval wheels. Add a character inside the car, leaning forward, and holding a wheel. Add the bumpers.

3. Drawing quickly, add two downward strokes behind the car and by each wheel. Draw horizontal lines from the back.

This race was outlined in pen and then painted using watercolors. The techniques described above were used to show the speed of all the racers.

A number was added to each racer, so they look like they are in an official race.

Blurred legs

1. Draw an oval head with long ears. Add a stick body leaning forward. Draw an oval on it. Add an arm and a tail.

2. Draw a scribbly oval where the legs would normally go. The legs are moving so fast they look like a blur.

3. Drawing quickly, add some motion lines at the bottom of the blurred legs. Then, add some little puffs of dust.

Sound effects

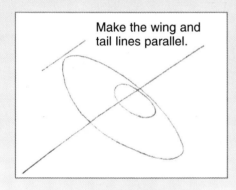

Make the wing and tail lines parallel.

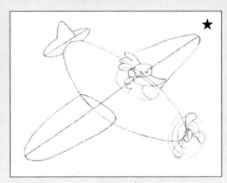

1. Draw an oval body for the plane. Add an oval cockpit. Pressing lightly, add diagonal lines for the wings and tail.

2. Outline the wings and tail. Add a character inside the cockpit. Add the propeller with scribbly circles on it.

3. Draw lines from the back of the plane. Then write 'zoom' inside the lines. Add motion lines behind the wings.

37

Stretching and squashing

In cartoons, characters and objects can be stretched or squashed to create various special effects. Cartoonists use squashing and stretching to show speed, weight or impact (something hitting something else).

A cartoon ball bouncing along squashes when it hits the floor and stretches when it lifts off again.

The speed at which this centipede is running is shown by all the slanted ovals.

The centipede is going so fast it isn't even touching the ground.

⟨☞ For links to websites where you can find short tutorials on how to draw things stretching and squashing, go to **www.usborne-quicklinks.com**

As the centipede hits a wall, its whole body squashes up.

Banana slip-up

The following step-by-steps show you how to draw the baby elephant from the comic strip on the next page.

Add a shadow beneath the elephant.

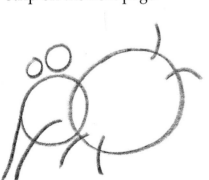

1. Draw an oval head. Add an oval body. Add big eyes and a long, curved trunk. Then, add stick arms and legs.

2. Put dots in the eyes. Add ears and a tail. Draw ovals on the ends of the legs and arms. Then, draw their outlines.

3. Draw the elephant's outline, adding toenails and other details. Draw a banana skin. Then, add some motion lines.

Make the head and the body ovals overlap.

Use a wavy line for the trunk.

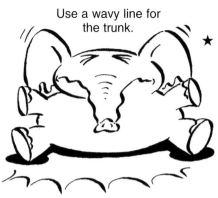

1. Draw a squashed oval head with a squashed oval body. Draw the eyes shut tight. Add stick arms and legs.

2. Draw a short trunk. Add triangular ears. Draw ovals on the ends of the arms and legs. Then, draw their outlines.

3. Add the toenails. Draw the elephant's outline. Fill in a shadow underneath. Then, add curved lines to show the impact.

This comic strip was drawn with permanent pen and painted with watercolors.

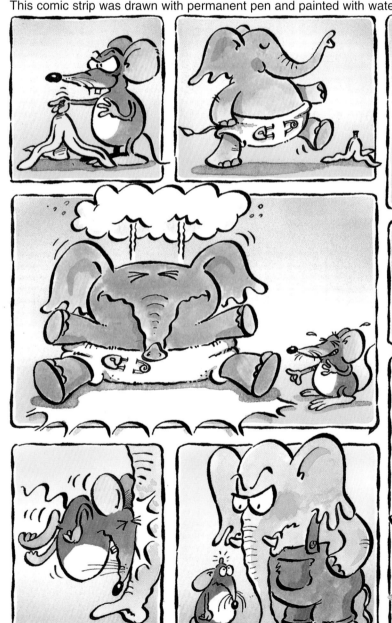

Cartoon antics

In the world of cartoons, anything can happen. Characters can fall off cliffs, or they can be flattened or stretched into all sorts of extraordinary shapes but be unhurt. Here are a few classic cartoon antics, to give you some ideas.

Dynamite

Cartoon dynamite doesn't actually hurt the characters. It just makes them turn black and sooty for a short while.

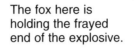

The fox here is holding the frayed end of the explosive.

Running off cliffs

The motion lines help to show his panicked movement.

If a cartoon character runs off a cliff, they will stay hanging in mid air until they notice there's no ground beneath them. Then, they will plummet to the ground very, very quickly.

Brick wall

If a character in a cartoon runs fast enough, they can go straight through a brick wall. They leave a hole shaped exactly like them behind.

Steamroller

If a character is rolled over by a steamroller, they will be flattened like a pancake and become taller than they were before. But, moments later they will spring back to their normal shape.

The moons and stars show that he's a little dazed.

Harebrained scheme

In lots of famous cartoons, one animal always chases after another, inventing more and more harebrained schemes to try to catch them. They never succeed. Here's how to draw a fox planning a crazy invention to catch a chicken.

For links to websites with step-by-step instructions for drawing cartoon special effects, and other cartoon attitudes and antics, go to **www.usborne-quicklinks.com**

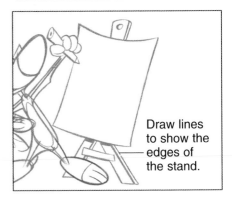

Draw lines to show the edges of the stand.

1. Draw a semicircle for a head. Add a snout, eyes and a mouth. Then, draw the body. Add stick legs and arms with oval paws.

2. Add ears, eyebrows and a tail. Draw a pencil, then add fingers on one paw. Then, draw the rest of the arms and legs.

3. For the easel, draw a rough rectangle for the board. Add the stand at the top and add the legs.

You could also use chalk or white pencil for drawing the plan.

4. Draw the 'plan' shown here on the board. Outline the scene in permanent pen, but leave the plan in pencil.

5. Color the scene using felt-tip pens or watercolors. Let it dry. Then, use correction fluid to go over the plan lines.

41

Perspective

The farther away things are from you the smaller they look. This is called perspective. There are tricks you can use to show perspective in your cartoons to make them look three-dimensional.

In this cartoon, the path gets smaller and smaller into the distance until you can't see it any more. The point at which it disappears from view is called the vanishing point.

Horses and a cowboy were added to make a Western street scene.

This is the vanishing point.

DRAW!!

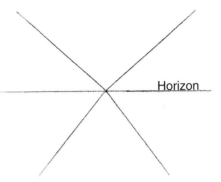

Horizon

1. Draw a horizontal line for the horizon. Then, add four slanted lines coming from one point on the horizon.

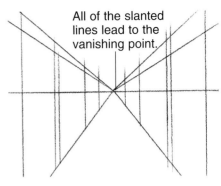

All of the slanted lines lead to the vanishing point.

2. Add vertical lines for the walls of each building. Add more slanted lines for the tops of the buildings.

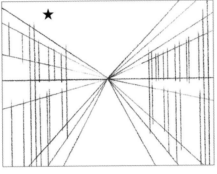

★

3. For the windows and doors, draw more slanted lines from the vanishing point. Then, add vertical lines for their sides.

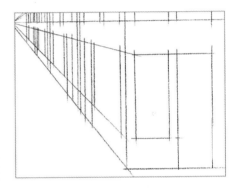

4. Draw horizontal lines for the fronts of the buildings on the street facing you. Add windows and doors.

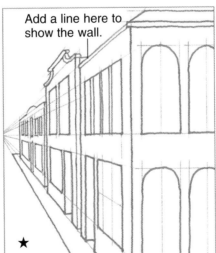

Add a line here to show the wall.

★

5. Add a pavement line and roofs to the buildings. Shape the doors, windows and fronts of the buildings.

6. Add frames around the windows and doors. You can add details, such as awnings on store fronts and tiles on roofs.

Skewed views

If you want to show something from a character's point of view, you can warp the drawing so that it looks like you are seeing it from a certain angle. This is another way of showing perspective (see page 42).

☞ For links to websites where you can follow step-by-step lessons on drawing in perspective and find tips on how to use perspective in your pictures, go to **www.usborne-quicklinks.com**

Worm's eye view

If you were very small and you looked up at a very tall person, such as this giant, his body would seem to get smaller and smaller the farther away from you it went.

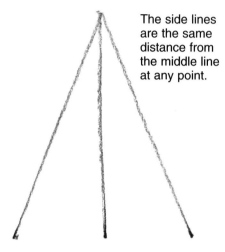

The side lines are the same distance from the middle line at any point.

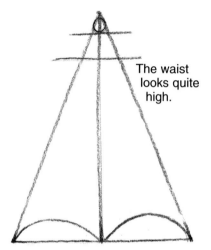

The waist looks quite high.

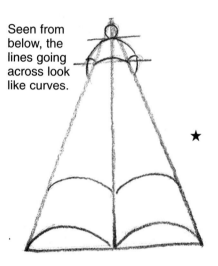

Seen from below, the lines going across look like curves.

★

1. Using pencil, draw a vertical line. Then, draw two diagonal lines coming from the same point at the top.

2. Draw two semicircles at the bottom. Then, mark a line for the waist and shoulders. Draw in a small circle for the head.

3. Add the arms, and draw the shirt sleeves. Draw the curved waist line and shoulder line. Add curved pants bottoms.

The eyes, nose and mouth are different shapes from underneath.

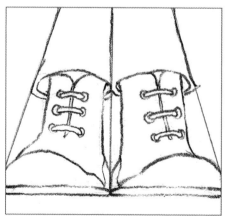

Finish off the bottoms of the pants.

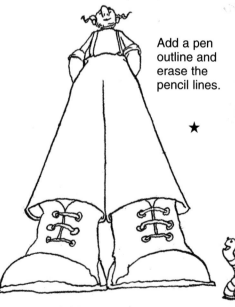

Add a pen outline and erase the pencil lines.

★

4. Draw eyes high on the head. Add the nose. Draw a mouth and add ears level with it. Add hairs on the chin and the head.

5. Add lines to show the soles of the shoes. Draw the sides of the boots. Add laces across and then draw the eyelets.

Add a small character whose viewpoint you are sharing.

44

Bird's eye view

If you could look down on a giant from above his head, his body would seem to get smaller and smaller, the further away from you it went.

The guidelines for drawing a person from a bird's eye view are the other way around from those for drawing a worm's eye view.

Mark where the shoulders and waist go before drawing the body.

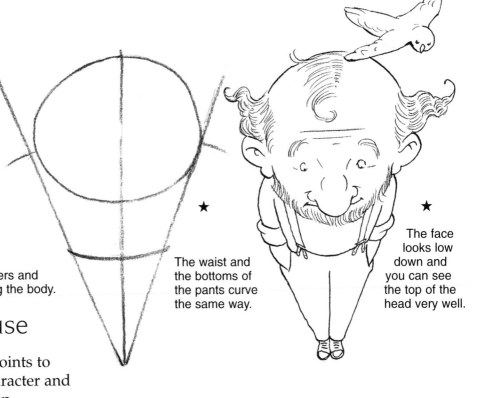

★ The waist and the bottoms of the pants curve the same way.

★ The face looks low down and you can see the top of the head very well.

A giant and a mouse

You can use these two viewpoints to alternate between a short character and a tall character in a comic strip.

Excuse me!

Excuse me!

You're standing on my tail!

Oh! I'm sorry little friend.

Wow! The world looks small from up here!

Superheroes

Superheroes have special powers, which can be anything from superhuman strength, to being able to fly or change their shape. They are normally seen battling villains. These pages give you a starting point for drawing superheroes of your own, which you can use in scenes with the villains on pages 48-49.

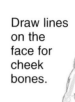

Drawing a superhero

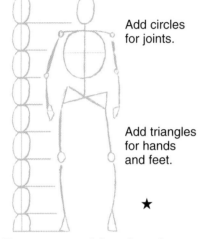

Add circles for joints.

Add triangles for hands and feet.

★

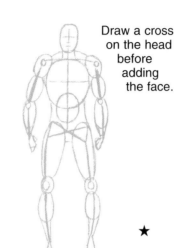

Draw a cross on the head before adding the face.

★

Draw lines on the face for cheek bones.

★

1. Draw an oval head and a stick body. Add an oval chest. Draw the hips, arms and legs. Make the figure eight and a half times its head height.

2. Add ovals for bulging muscles to the arms and legs. Add an oval for the stomach muscles. Outline the shoulders and waist.

3. Go over the outline. Draw the face. Add gloves, boots and pants. Add dark areas for shading in the places shown here to emphasize his muscles.

Poses

The secret to making superheroes look dramatic and exciting, is to draw them in very exaggerated poses. The stick men below show some action poses you could use.

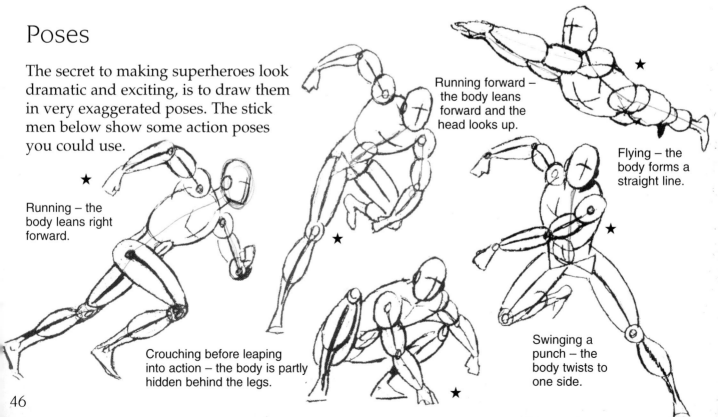

★

Running – the body leans right forward.

Running forward – the body leans forward and the head looks up.

★

Flying – the body forms a straight line.

★

Crouching before leaping into action – the body is partly hidden behind the legs.

★

Swinging a punch – the body twists to one side.

★

For links to websites where you can read superhero comics online and watch a video clip lesson on how to draw a cartoon superhero, go to www.usborne-quicklinks.com

See page 49 for how to draw this villain.

47

Villains

Bad guys in action cartoons can be anything from evil scientists, to power-hungry businessmen or enormous swamp monsters. Here are some ideas for drawing villains.

For links to websites where you can explore picture galleries of famous cartoon villains, go to www.usborne-quicklinks.com

Evil scientist

An evil scientist has a skinny, hunched body. He is an old man wearing a lab coat.

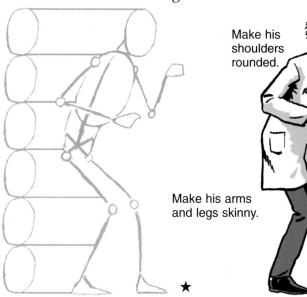

Make his shoulders rounded.

Make his arms and legs skinny.

★

Draw the hunched figure six heads high.

Add a test tube and a lab coat to show he is a scientist.

A sneaky scientist might look over his shoulder like this.

A scientist might grin, forming an evil plan.

A cowardly villain might gasp with fear.

Power-hungry businessman

The power-hungry businessman has a squat body. He is middle-aged and wears a pin-striped suit.

Make his arms and legs chunky.

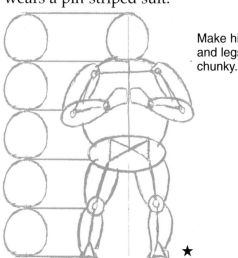

A greedy villain might fling his arms out when saying he wanted to take over the world!

★

★

Draw the figure five heads high.

Add big, square-shaped hands.

An evil villain might laugh in triumph.

An evil villain might scowl with fury.

Swamp monster

Monsters can take any shape you like. This swamp monster has a bulky, muscular body. Its head sinks low into its shoulders. It is covered in slime.

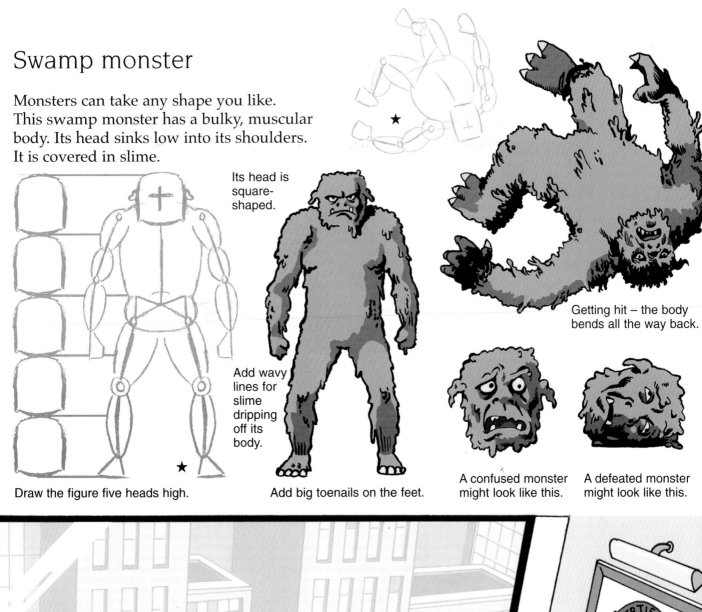

Its head is square-shaped.

Add wavy lines for slime dripping off its body.

Draw the figure five heads high.

Add big toenails on the feet.

Getting hit – the body bends all the way back.

A confused monster might look like this.

A defeated monster might look like this.

To draw the villains in a scene, draw them in pencil first and then add the background.

Animation

Moving cartoons, or animations, are made by showing still pictures very quickly one after the other. They are shown so quickly that your eye is fooled into thinking it sees a moving picture. To make a film, animators have to create every single picture that will be shown.

This is a still picture from the cartoon *Popeye*. It shows Olive Oyl and Popeye dancing.

©King Features Syndicate

Flip book

To make a flip book you need a pad of paper which is thin enough to see through slightly. By drawing the same character over and over again, but changing its position a little each time, you can make it look as if it is moving.

★ Instead of drawing these frogs you can download them to make a flip book. To do this, go to **www.usborne-quicklinks.com**

1. Using quite dark pencil or felt-tip pen, draw a character on the back page of the pad in the bottom, right-hand corner.

2. Flip the next page on top and draw the character again, but in a slightly different position from the first time.

3. Flip to the next page. Draw the character on this page again, moving its position a little more.

4. Flip the next page on top. Draw the character again, remembering to only change the position slightly each time.

5. Continue flipping the pages over and drawing the character in a slightly different position on each of the pages.

6. Flip through the pages from the back of the pad to the front. The character will seem to be moving.

Stages of animation

An animation has to go through lots of stages before becoming a finished cartoon. The pictures below show the different stages one drawing would go through before becoming a part of an animation.

The final outline is drawn in black.

★

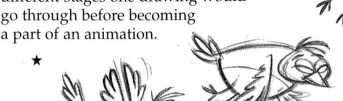

First of all, 'roughs' are drawn to work out the character.

Next, the bird is drawn in blue pencil to get the position perfect.

The finished cartoon is colored in.

Making a storyboard

Before making an animation, an animator will sketch out a story to show what happens. This is called making a storyboard. A storyboard looks like a comic strip, showing only the main actions. To make a storyboard, think of a story and then sketch it out in frames.

For links to websites where you can watch animated flick books, take an online animation tutorial and make your own short animations online, go to **www.usborne-quicklinks.com** You can also peek behind the scenes at how animated films are made and learn how to create characters and storyboards of your own.

You can use a storyboard to plan out a much longer animation than one you can make in a flip book.

Sound effects (SFX) for the actual cartoon are suggested in writing below the frames.

SFX - GUNSHOT

HA HA!

CRASH!! OOF!!

TWEET TWEET

CLICK

51

Computer drawing

Many modern cartoons are drawn on computer. If you have a computer with Microsoft® Windows® on it, it will have a program called Paint, which you can use for drawing cartoons. Usually, you can open the program by following the steps below.

Opening Paint

1. Using your mouse, position the pointer over the *Start* button and click (using the left mouse button). A list will pop up on your screen.

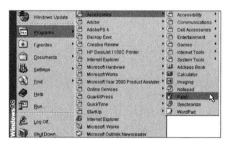

2. Move your pointer over the word *Programs*. Another list will appear. Move the pointer to *Accessories*. On the list that appears, click on *Paint*.

3. A box, or window, will appear. The white area in the middle is a page that you can draw on. There are tools for drawing around the edge.

Paint tools

To draw you first need to choose a tool. To do this, position your pointer over a tool in the tool box and click on it. You may see options below the tool box, which you can click on, too. To choose a colour, click on a colored square in the paint box.

This is the tool box.

If you click on the brush tool in the tool box, these options appear beneath. Click on one to choose a style and size of brush to use.

This is the paint box.

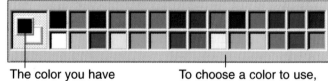

The color you have chosen appears here.

To choose a color to use, click on a colored square.

Drawing freehand

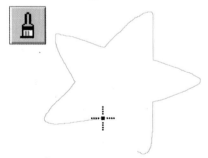

Click on the brush tool. Move the pointer to the page. Pressing the left mouse button down, drag the mouse to draw.

Filling in

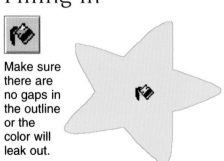

Make sure there are no gaps in the outline or the color will leak out.

Click on the paint can. Click on a color. Move the pointer over a shape and click to fill the shape with color.

Erasing

Click on the eraser. Pressing the left mouse button down, drag the pointer over whatever you want to erase.

This scene was created using the tools described on these pages.

The spines on this puffer fish were drawn using the odd shape tool.

Select the brush tool and click to make dots in the eyes.

See page 56 for how to undo any mistakes you make.

Drawing ovals

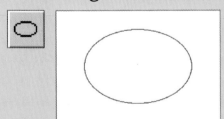

Click on the oval tool. Move the pointer over the page. Pressing the left mouse button, drag the mouse to draw an oval. Let go of the mouse button to finish the shape.

Odd shapes

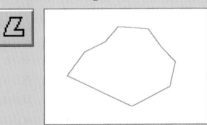

Click on the odd shape tool. Pressing the left mouse button, drag the mouse to draw a side. Let the button go, then press and drag to make another side. Double-click to finish the shape.

Shape options

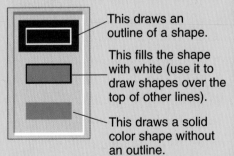

This draws an outline of a shape.

This fills the shape with white (use it to draw shapes over the top of other lines).

This draws a solid color shape without an outline.

When you click on a shape tool, these three options appear beneath the tool box. Click on one to choose it.

Computer cartoons

You can add words to pictures in Microsoft® Paint. You can use this to add speech bubbles to computer cartoons. These pages show you how to draw a cartoon with a speech bubble. Look at pages 52-53 if you need help using some of the tools.

Draw a tortoise

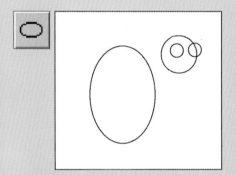

1. Click on the oval tool. Then, pressing the left mouse button, drag the pointer to draw a body, a head and two eyes.

2. Click on the brush tool. Click on a small brush style option. Draw the neck and nose. Add eyebrows and dots in the eyes.

Add toenails on the feet.

3. Draw the edge of the tortoise's shell and then add lines on its body. Add arms, legs and a tail.

Make sure there aren't gaps in the outline before you fill it in.

4. Click on the eraser. Erase any extra lines. Click on the paint can and click on a color. Click on the tortoise to fill it in.

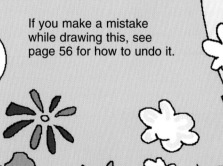

Hurray! Hurray!

If you make a mistake while drawing this, see page 56 for how to undo it.

Add a speech bubble

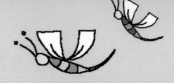

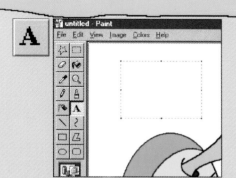

1. To add words, first click on the A tool. Pressing the left mouse button, drag the mouse to make a dotted box.

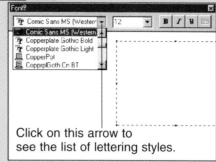

Click on this arrow to see the list of lettering styles.

2. A 'Fonts' box will appear. It allows you to choose how the lettering will look. Click on the arrow to see a list.

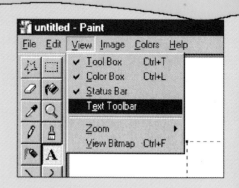

3. If the Fonts box doesn't appear, click on *View* at the top of the window. On the list that appears, click on *Text Toolbar*.

These words were written using a lettering style called Comic Sans MS.

I'm winning!

4. Click on an option in the list to choose a style of lettering. Then click in the dotted box. Type some words.

These words were written using size 10.

I'm winning!

5. To change the letter size, click on the number in the Fonts box. Type a lower or higher number, then click inside the dotted box.

The dotted box around the words will disappear.

I'm winning!

6. Click outside the dotted box to finish your lettering. It will become part of the picture, so you can't change it any more.

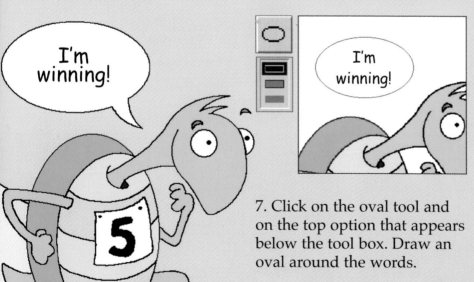

7. Click on the oval tool and on the top option that appears below the tool box. Draw an oval around the words.

8. Click on the brush. Click on a small brush style option below the tool box. Add a tail to the oval. Erase the extra line.

Computer comic strips

An advantage of using a computer to draw a comic strip is that there are tools you can use to copy a character, so it can appear again without you having to redraw it. Here are some tips for drawing a comic strip on computer.

Drawing frames

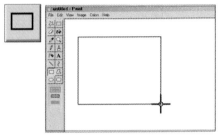

Click on the rectangle tool. Pressing the left mouse button down, drag the mouse to draw a rectangular frame.

Undo mistakes

If you make a mistake, hold CTRL down on your keyboard and press the Z key. This deletes the last thing you did.

Draw a mouse

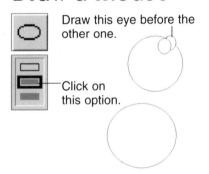

Draw this eye before the other one.

Click on this option.

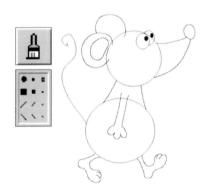

Make sure there are no gaps in the outline before you fill it in.

1. Click on the oval tool. Then, click on the middle option under the tool box. Draw ovals for the head, body and eyes.

2. Click on the brush and on a small brush style. Draw ears and a nose. Add pupils in the eyes. Draw the rest of the body.

3. Click on the eraser tool. Erase any extra lines. Click on the paint can and click on a color. Click on the drawing to fill it in.

To draw this comic strip, first draw some frames and then use the tips above to draw the mouse in different positions.

Draw and color the cheese and the backgrounds last.

56

Making a copy

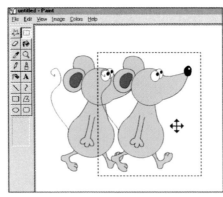
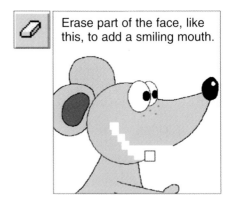

1. Click on the select tool. Click on the bottom option under the tool box. Pressing the left mouse button, drag a box around the drawing.

2. Position your pointer in the box and, holding the CTRL key down on your keyboard, drag the box. It will make a copy. Click outside the box.

3. You can drag the copy into another frame in your strip, and then change it. Use the eraser, brush and paint can tools to alter the picture.

Turning heads

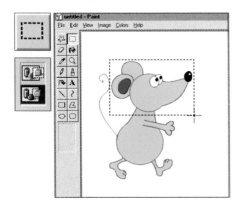
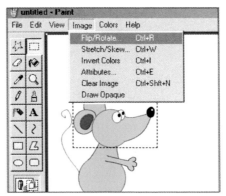
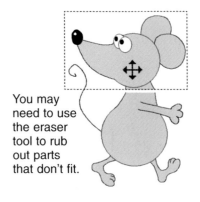

1. Click on the select tool. Click on the bottom option under the tool box. Pressing the left mouse button, drag a box around the mouse's head.

2. Click on *Image* at the top of the window. A list will appear. Click on *Flip/Rotate*. A box will appear. Click in the dot by *Flip horizontal*, and then click on *OK*.

3. The mouse's head will flip over. Pressing the left mouse button down, drag the head so it fits onto the body. Click outside the box to fix it in place.

Find out how to add a speech bubble on page 55.
Add the bubble before you color the background.

★

57

Drawing from life

To get cartoon ideas for how people stand, how they act or look in certain situations, it is a good idea to keep a little sketchbook with you. Make quick drawings of people around you at bus stops, in shopping centers, in parks or playgrounds.

Try to draw quick cartoons of the way people run.

Don't worry about drawing very accurately, sometimes a rough sketch can show more character.

Do scribbly drawings of the things people do while waiting for a bus.

People standing at a bus stop can look bored, cold, relaxed or tense.

If you are drawing someone close up, make sure you ask their permission first.

Making faces

Many cartoonists keep a mirror by their drawing board. If they want to draw a cartoon of someone showing a particular emotion, and need to see what it would look like, they make a face showing that emotion in the mirror. If you have a camera, you can also take pictures of friends making exaggerated faces to use as reference.

For links to websites where you can find tips on how to sketch figures and faces, see lots of funny caricatures of famous people and make a mini-cartoon online, go to **www.usborne-quicklinks.com**

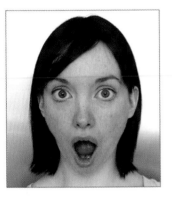 

When someone is surprised, their eyebrows go up and their mouth opens wide.

When someone is grimacing, one eye shuts and their mouth slants to one side.

When someone is gleeful, their eyebrows go up and their mouth makes an open curve.

When someone is feeling thoughtful, they might look up and to one side.

When someone is shouting, their mouth opens very wide.

If someone feels suspicious, one eyebrow goes up and the other goes down.

59

Gallery

Over the next four pages you can see a gallery of cartoons, which were drawn or painted using techniques and materials described in this book. Look through the gallery for new ideas. You can turn back to the pages mentioned to read more about certain techniques.

Cartoon sausage dogs can be made extra long, like this one. (See pages 16-17 for more dog characters.)

This giraffe was drawn using permanent pen and watercolor (see page 22).

The balloons were painted on damp paper letting the colors blur together (see page 22).

These people were drawn using ideas from pages 8-11. They were outlined in permanent pen and painted using watercolors (see pages 22-23).

For links to websites where you can meet *Bugs Bunny*, *Mickey Mouse*, the *Disney Princesses* and many other cartoon characters, go to **www.usborne-quicklinks.com**

The motion lines on these monkeys show that they are swinging (see page 36).

These people all have different-shaped faces (see pages 8-9). The scene was colored using an effect similar to those described on page 26.

This boy was drawn in 'Manga' style. Manga is a Japanese comic book style.

This spider was painted using watercolors (see page 22).

Lines have been added here to show the impact of the girl kicking the ball (see pages 36-39).

This character looks a bit squashed because he's fallen over (see pages 38-39).

These shadows were created using shadow and color effects like those on pages 21 and 26.

61

These hares were drawn on computer, using a program called Microsoft® Paint (see pages 52-57).

This speeding car has motion lines and puffs of smoke to show how fast it is going. You can see how to do these techniques on pages 36-37.

These faces were drawn showing different expressions (see page 6 and page 59).

This was drawn using pen and then painted using watercolors (see page 22).

This monster was drawn as an oval shape with arms and legs. It was painted with watercolors, using light and dark shades for the fur.

A fairground can make an exciting setting for a comic strip. This wall was drawn showing perspective (see page 42-43).

☞ For links to websites where you can visit more cartoon sites including *The Simpsons*, and explore a timeline of Disney movies, with video clips and pictures of classic cartoons, go to **www.usborne-quicklinks.com**

★ The clothes this man is wearing show that he is a cowboy (see page 12).

A castle is a good setting for a spooky cartoon. This scene uses color effects to make it look spookier (see page 26).

★ This cat was drawn using a similar technique to the animal characters on pages 16-17.

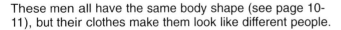

These men all have the same body shape (see page 10-11), but their clothes make them look like different people.

This girl was drawn over and over in different positions to show her movements. This technique can be used in a comic, or in animation (see pages 50-51).

★

America Speaks
THE BIRTH OF THE NATION

VOLUME
2

PRODUCERS

Wayne Youngblood

GROLIER

First published in the United States in 2005 by
Grolier, a division of Scholastic Library Publishing,
Sherman Turnpike, Danbury, CT 06816

For Compendium Publishing
Series editor: Don Gulbrandsen
Picture research: Sandra Forty
Design: Tony Stocks/Compendium Design
Artwork: Mark Franklin

Printed in China through Printworks Int. Ltd.

Library of Congress Cataloging-in-Publication Data
   p. cm.
Summary: "Recounts the making of America until 1815 through
the eyes and voices of ordinary people"—Provided by publisher.
Includes indexes.

Contents: v. 1. Merchants / Angus Konstam—v. 2.
Manufacturers / Wayne Youngblood—v. 3. Armed Forces / Ian
Westwell—v. 4. Transporters / John Westwood—v. 5.
Professionals / Marcus Cowper—v. 6. Workers / Marcus Cowper
—v. 7. Underprivileged / Duncan Clarke—v. 8. Lawmen and
Lawbreakers / Philip Wilkinson—v. 9. Women / Jane Penrose—
v. 10. Children / Jane Penrose.

ISBN 0-7172-6030-5 (set : alk. paper)—ISBN 0-7172-6020-8 (v. 1
: alk. paper)—ISBN 0-7172-6021-6 (v. 2 : alk. paper)—ISBN 0-
7172-6022-4 (v. 3 : alk. paper)—ISBN 0-7172-6023-2 (v. 4 : alk.
paper)—ISBN 0-7172-6024-0 (v. 5 : alk. paper)—ISBN 0-7172-
6025-9 (v. 6 : alk. paper)—ISBN 0-7172-6026-7 (v. 7 : alk. paper)
—ISBN 0-7172-6027-5 (v. 8 : alk. paper)—ISBN 0-7172-6028-3
(v. 9 : alk. paper)—ISBN 0-7172-6029-1 (v. 10 : alk. paper)

1. United States—History—Colonial period, ca. 1600-1775—
Sources—Juvenile literature. 2. United States--History—
Revolution, 1775-1783—Sources—Juvenile literature. 3. United
States—History—1783-1815—Sources—Juvenile literature. 4.
United States—Social conditions—To 1865—Sources—
Juvenile literature. I. Konstam, Angus.

E188.A495 2005
973.2'5—dc22

2005040309

ACKNOWLEDGMENTS

The photographs in this book came
from the following sources. Numbers
refer to pages

Author's collection: 28B, 52B, 63.
Corbis: 1 (Bettmann/Corbis), 3C & B
(Bettmann/Corbis and Gianni Dagli
Orti/Corbis), 4 (Bettmann/Corbis, Gianni
Dagli Orti/Corbis, & Bettmann/Corbis), 5
(Kelly-Mooney Photography/Corbis), 6
(Stapleton Collection/Corbis), 7 (Gianni
Dagli Orti/Corbis), 8 (both Lowell
Georgia/Corbis), 9 (Bettmann/Corbis),
10 (Bettmann/Corbis), 11A, 14A, 16, 17
(Bettmann/Corbis), 18 (Historical
Picture Archive/Corbis), 19 (Stapleton
Collection/Corbis and Lee Snider/Photo
Images/Corbis), 20 (Bettmann/Corbis
and Corbis), 23 (Lowell Georgia/Corbis),
24B (Corbis), 25 (Bettmann/Corbis), 26
(Bettmann/Corbis), 27B, 28, 29 (Richard
T. Nowitz/Corbis), 30 (Bettmann/Corbis),
31 (Historical Picture Archive/Corbis and
Bettmann/Corbis), 34 (Bettmann/Corbis
and Stapleton Collection/Corbis), 36, 37
(Historical Picture Archive/Corbis), 38
(Elio Ciol/Corbis), 39, 40A (Lee
Snider/Photo Images/Corbis), 43, 45
(Bettmann/Corbis), 46, 48A (Historical
Picture Archive/Corbis), 49 (Kirsten
Soderlind/Corbis), 50 (both), 52A
(Bettmann/Corbis), 53 (The Mariners'
Museum/Corbis), 54 (Francis G.
Mayer/Corbis), 55 (Bettmann/Corbis),
56, 57A (Bettmann/Corbis), 59 (all
Bettmann/Corbis), 60 (Francis G.
Mayer/Corbis and Corbis), 62A (Joseph
Sohm; ChromoSohm Inc./Corbis),
64 (Bettmann/Corbis), 65 (Christel
Gerstenberg/Corbis), 66, 67 (Bettmann/
Corbis), 68 (Bettmann/Corbis and Corbis
SYGMA), 69 (Bettmann/ Corbis),
70 (Bettmann/Corbis), 71 (Philip Gould/
Corbis), 72 (Richard Cummins/Corbis).
David Lyons: 14B.
Getty Images: 3T, 11B, 12, 22 (both),
24A, 27, 35, 40B, 41, 42, 44, 46B, 47,
48B, 57BL & BR, 58, 61, 73.

CONTENTS

The story of the producers in America covers many areas, including heavy industry (iron smelting and milling), agricultural products (tobacco, cotton, indigo, and rice), products made in America for use in trading elsewhere (rum), and industries related to America's vast wealth of natural resources (furs, fish, naval stores, and shipbuilding). Some of these industries, such as tobacco and fishing, developed during the earliest colonial days. Others, such as textile factories, didn't begin until after the end of the Revolutionary War. One very important but unintended aspect of the success of America is the diversification of these industries. When one type of industry had problems, others were there to take its place.

The principle of mercantilism

At the central core of the founding and much of the history of manufacturing during America's colonial years is the principle of mercantilism. What exactly is mercantilism? Mercantilism, in

RIGHT: **A musical instrument craftsman carves a violin neck by hand at Anthony Hay's cabinetmaking shop in historic Colonial Williamsburg, Virginia.**

FAR LEFT: **This engraving shows an Englishman receiving tobacco from an Indian, via his slave.**

LEFT: **A slave dressed in traditional African garb.**

BELOW LEFT: **Tobacco as it has been grown in Virginia and Maryland for more than 350 years. Tobacco is harvested today by the same methods used in the days of Sir Walter Raleigh, who was the first to popularize the weed in England.**

simple terms, holds that a country's power and financial base can be greatly expanded by establishing colonies. These colonies (assumed to be rich in natural resources) provide the raw materials needed by the country to manufacture various types of finished products. These products are then sold back to the colonies (as well as the population of the country itself), enriching both (especially the country). The notion of mercantilism also somehow developed—at least in the founding of America—that these colonies could also take unwanted people from the country, including the poor, orphans, and criminals, and put them to profitable and effective use.

In requesting children from the city of London to be sent to the New World as indentured laborers, the Virginia Company wrote about those children:

> "Of whome the city is especially desireous to be disburdened, and in Virginia under severe masters they may be brought to goodness."

The Virginia Company saw the children as a source of cheap labor, but people soon started to believe that the New World could serve as an effective "reform school." An unintended consequence was that a thriving child market soon developed in London, in which innocent children were lured or simply stolen by ships setting sail for America.

The colonists

Around the time the first colonists were headed for Jamestown, the mayor of Bristol told the king that those who left England were:

5

"Unruly gallants packed thither by their friends to escape ill destines…condemned wretches, forfeited by law…poor gentlemen, broken tradesmen, rakes and libertines, footmen and such others fitter to spoil or ruin a commonwealth than to help raise and maintain one."

While this negative view was true for some who sought their fortune in America, it does not describe the majority of people who wanted to pursue a new life across the ocean. The colonists included those who wanted to worship in peace, adventurers who longed to explore the unknown, and those who wished to start a new trade.

A more optimistic person of the same era made the statement that:

"God sifted an whole nation that He might bring choice grain over into this wilderness."

Whatever their backgrounds, colonists who set foot onto the New World were arguably disproportionately represented by creative and innovative types. Of those who founded Massachusetts (300 heads of households), only 75 were farmers. The remaining settlers, mostly from cities, were skilled brewers, shoe-makers, coopers (barrel makers), tailors, weavers, metalworkers, and other tradesmen.

America, it seemed, was from the beginning destined to become an innovative manufacturing center. It was able to thrive and grow—to some extent "under the radar"—because of England's inaccurate and somewhat condescending view of the colonists.

A free market

As the colonies and their respective profits grew, money came to signify an individual's moral and practical victory over nature and circumstance—never mind, of course, that much of that money was made at the expense of others. For several generations after the initial colonization of America a growing desire for a free market was in direct conflict with attempts to regulate the colonial economy and manufacturing system. The authorities in England and American religious movements were both responsible for these attempts to control American free enterprise. A revolution was probably inevitable at some point.

Tobacco and slavery

As you'll read in the following chapters, most of the different types of early American industry are interwoven in various ways. One unfortunate but dominant theme throughout is the reliance of early Americans on involuntary or slave labor. It is particularly ironic that the early success and wealth of America (on which most later success was built) would not have been possible without two institutions many Americans would rather not acknowledge: tobacco and slavery.

Tobacco continues to be a profitable industry, but most Americans are not proud of this because of the health problems caused by smoking and chewing tobacco. Nonetheless, it was the savior of the early starving settlers in Virginia and became this country's earliest major export product.

Likewise, slave labor was an important and integral part of most of the farming in the colonies, including tobacco, rice, indigo, and cotton. Slaves were used for running the iron furnaces that eventually produced the shackles that bound them. They labored in the huge southern forests to produce the

BELOW: **An illustration of an Atlantic salmon by Johan Friedrich August Krueger and Johan Friedrich Henning, 1785. Salmon and cod played an important part in the early colonial economy.**

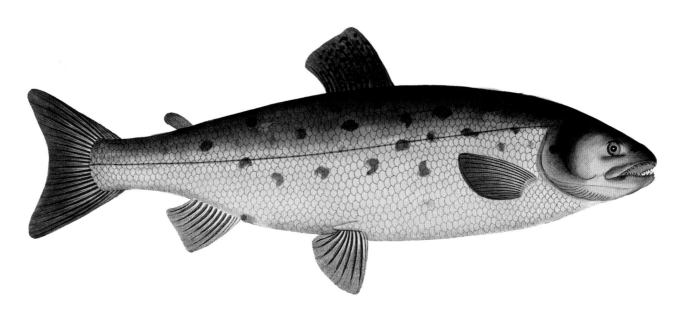

the iron industry, and distilling, to grow and thrive.

Natural resources

Another common thread that weaves its way through the colonial history of the manufacturers is the waste and depletion of rich natural resources.

Early tobacco planters simply cleared more land and moved on when soil became "used up." No thought was given to the numbers of fur-bearing animals that were—at first—plentiful, then disappeared from "civilized" areas. Millions of acres of virgin woods (with monster-sized trees) were deforested. While much of this wood was utilized, a vast amount was simply burned to get it "out of the way." No thought was given to replacing the forests used for shipbuilding, dwellings, iron smelting, and naval stores. As a result, some of the markets changed during individual lifetimes due to once-common resources growing scarcer. The colonists weren't bad people; they simply did not understand the effect they had on their surroundings and felt that the natural resources of the air, earth, and water were limitless. They were, unfortunately, wrong.

The fishing, whaling, and fur industries all relied heavily on abundant native animals, and each changed as areas were fished or hunted out. Cod was thought to be an inexhaustible food source for all of the colonies and Europe, and is still common. Beaver pelts were among the earliest fur in demand due to a style fad in Europe. But the near decimation of fur-bearing animals near the coast led to more expansion and exploration of the inland.

lumber and naval stores (forest products such as turpentine, tar, and pitch used in shipbuilding) to build the ships that would eventually bring more of their countrymen to the same fate. Slaves did all this work while others—including fellow Africans who conspired with traders—were profiting. There were even free blacks who were slave owners themselves and felt the economic pressure to maintain the terribly unfair system.

What made the slave system even more possible (and successful) is what is known as the Golden Triangle. Our

innovative forefathers discovered very early that an extremely profitable trade could be developed between America, Africa, and the West Indies. Slaves were brought over to the West Indies, where most were either sold or traded for the cheap slave-produced molasses. This molasses, as well as the remaining slaves, were brought to the colonies where they were sold or traded for New England rum. Then, vessels loaded with rum headed for Africa to trade for more slaves. This highly successful and profitable triangle allowed other colonial American trades, such as shipbuilding,

CANDLE MAKING

A living history program in Oregon relives the life and times of early 1800s pioneers for visitors to the Fort Clatsop National Memorial. The staff member shown above is dressed in traditional buckskin and demonstrates how to make candles. He is shown here putting a wick into brass candle mold. Various forms of candles provided most of the evening light for colonial Americans.

The Industrial Revolution

Toward the end of the colonial period and American Revolution another revolution was beginning: the Industrial Revolution. This warless revolution, which would take America from a primarily agriculturally based economy to one much more closely tied to manufacturing, was no less controversial than the Revolutionary War.

The proponents of this type of progress included George Washington, Alexander Hamilton, and others. They felt that a solid manufacturing base would help America grow financially as an emerging country. It would also help keep the country independent and less reliant on foreign imports in an always-changing and often-unfriendly world. In Hamilton's 1791 *Report on Manufactures* he argued passionately that the new government needed to take an active financial role to help manufacturing—and the country—flourish:

"In countries where there is great private wealth much may be effected by the voluntary contributions of patriotic individuals, but in a community situated like that of the United States, the public purse must supply the deficiency of private resource. In what can it be so useful as in prompting and improving the efforts of industry?"

Opponents of this movement, including Thomas Jefferson, felt that America

should continue to focus on agriculture and the rich natural resources that made various types of farming so highly successful and profitable. Of course, Jefferson's calculations didn't include the considerable—but involuntary—contributions of well over a half-million slaves who were at that time laboring in his and numerous other fields. Jefferson also felt strongly that manufacturers would introduce negative moral and behavioral influences that would become a significant problem for the country over time. Jefferson summarized his beliefs in the 1780s in his *Notes on Virginia*:

"Those who labor in the earth are the chosen people of God, if ever he had a chosen people, whose breasts he has made his peculiar deposit for substantial and genuine virtue. It is the focus in which he keeps alive that sacred fire, which otherwise might escape from the face of the earth. Corruption of morals in the mass of cultivators is a phenomenon of which no age nor nation has furnished an example."

The other main reason for opposing the Industrial Revolution is one that has been faced by various cultures for centuries and one that continues to be controversial in America today: With each new invention or labor-saving innovation jobs are lost. Generally they are more than made up for by the needs for new skills connected to these innovations, but the fear is that skilled craftsmen and other workers will no longer be needed.

Printing

While we know that history has generally proven these fears to be false, something is indeed lost with invention. You need look no further than the printing industry for evidence of this. The first products from America's presses were

crude publications, but a true pride and artistic skill soon developed. Truly fine printed works are a rich part of our heritage.

Books, pamphlets, and other printed works were scarce for colonists and were held dear; those same products are now easily accessible to all. But they are no longer lovingly hand-bound volumes printed on high-quality paper with rich engravings. Most are reproduced

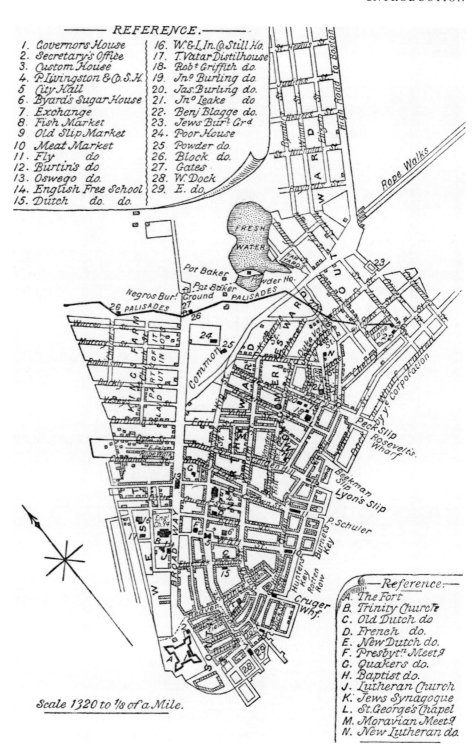

REFERENCE.

1. Governors House
2. Secretary's Office
3. Custom House
4. P. Livingston & Co. S.H.
5. City Hall
6. Byard's Sugar House
7. Exchange
8. Fish Market
9. Old Slip Market
10. Meat Market
11. Fly   do
12. Burtin's do
13. Oswego   do
14. English Free School
15. Dutch   do. do.
16. W. & L. In. @ Still Ho.
17. T. Vatar Distilhouse
18. Robt Griffith do.
19. Jno Burling do.
20. Jas. Burling do.
21. Jno Leake do.
22. Benj Blagge do.
23. Jews Burl Grd
24. Poor House
25. Powder do.
26. Block do.
27. Gates
28. W. Dock
29. E. do.

Reference:
A. The Fort
B. Trinity Church
C. Old Dutch do
D. French do.
E. New Dutch do.
F. Presbytn Meetg
G. Quakers do.
H. Baptist do.
J. Lutheran Church
K. Jews Synagogue
L. St. George's Chapel
M. Moravian Meetg
N. New Lutheran do.

Scale 1320 to 1/8 of a Mile.

ABOVE: **This map of New York City from the mideighteenth century shows the developed tip of Manhattan and open farmland up to today's 42nd Street. The key at upper left identifies important locations such as the governor's house, Exchange, markets, etc.; the key at lower right shows the main churches that existed at the time.**

LEFT: **Children working in a factory.**

quickly on thin, machine-made paper with stitched or glued bindings that aren't terribly durable. Nonetheless, these items, such as the one you're holding now, are available to everyone.

These printed works inform and educated "the masses"—and that lies at the core of a successful democracy. Most agree that it is a worthwhile trade.

As we reach the occasion of the 400th anniversary of the permanent settlement of America, we have a natu-

ABOVE: **This etching depicts the bustling Manhattan waterfront as it appeared around the beginning of the eighteenth century.**

BELOW: **Virginia explorer William Clark and his men are shown shooting bears in this engraving.**

ral landmark to make us stop, look back, and take a moment to reflect. That is what you'll read here: a celebration and reflection of what it took to build America during its first 200 years.

The development of industry

In the chapters that follow, you'll trace each industry from its infancy through the end of the Revolutionary War and slightly beyond in some cases. Many of these industries share common patterns of development, which to some extent simply reflect the developmental stages of the colonies. Dale Taylor, in his book *Everyday Life in Colonial America, 1607-1783* refers to three distinct colonial periods: The Period of Settlement (roughly 1607-75), when basic colonization and survival issues were addressed; the Period of Organization (roughly 1675–1750), when the colonies began to grow and gained financial and political strength; and the Period of Revolution, ending in about 1783, which deals more specifically with the struggle for independence from Britain's heavy-handed rule. While not all of these industries can trace their histories so neatly, some follow this pattern closely. Those that do—primarily the agricultural products—also are tied to their respective geographical areas.

In the chapter on tobacco, for example, initial cultivation (in Virginia) developed from the need to survive, leading to a profitable and marketable crop that eventually came under British scrutiny until after the war. Both the iron and rum industries were successful early on and were eventually limited by the British (by various acts and tariffs) due to their success, until after the Revolution.

Other industries, such as naval stores, thrived from early on and were actually spurred on by the needs of the war effort. The printing industry (more specifically publishing) grew out of the public's need to be informed. Still other industries, however, such as cotton and the textile mills, didn't fully get their start until after the Revolutionary War.

All colonial industries shared a common bond: The development of each filled an important need (physical, financial, or cultural) of the American people.

BELOW: **An American family is shown trampling grapes and using a wine press to make wine on a Virginia farm during the seventeenth century. However, colonial wines produced from both native and imported grapes proved commercially unsuccessful at the time.**

TOBACCO

"Tobacco that outlandish weede
It spends the braine and spoiles the seede
It dulls the spirite, it dims the sight
It robs a woman of her right"

So goes a rhyme written by Dr. William Vaughn in 1617. This leafy crop, which rapidly became popular in England after its introduction by early New World explorers, was already controversial by the early seventeenth century. But Vaughn's view of tobacco was not shared by those who used it. In fact, smoking tobacco was thought by many to cure all ills. Thomas Hariot, writing *A Brief and True Report of the New Found Land of Virginia* in 1588, made the following notation:

> "The fumes purge superfluous phlem and gross humors from the body by opening all the pores and passages. Thus its use not only preserves the body, but if there are any obstructions, it breaks them up. By this means the natives keep in excellent health without many of the grievous diseases which afflict us in England."

An early tobacco label described the "beneficial weed" as follows:

> "Hail thou inspiring plant! Thou balm of life,

LEFT: **Farmers inside a tobacco curing house.**

BELOW LEFT: **Cured tobacco leaves.**

BELOW: **Map showing tobacco-growing states.**

Well might thy worth engage two nations' strife;
Exhaustless fountain of Britannia's wealth;
Thou friend of wisdom and thou source of health."

And a seventeenth-century song, "Tobacco is Like Love," sang its praises: "Love makes men sail from shore to shore…so doth tobacco."

A blessing and a curse

America as we know it likely would not exist if it wasn't for tobacco—an unintentional crop that proved to be both a blessing and a curse to the colonies. In fact, no other crop in recorded history has had such a direct effect on the survival and growth of a culture.

When the Jamestown settlers arrived, they were not prepared for the harsh life of the New World. Malaria, Indian attacks, bitter cold, disease, and drought killed many colonists. By the spring of 1609 few original colonists were still alive. One thing the hardy survivors noticed was that Native Americans used wild tobacco that grew readily in the area. Because tobacco was already popular in England, it became clear that growing tobacco might be an answer to their prayers.

Early cultivation was from Spanish seed, and the colonists learned that drying leaves under shaded roofs produced a milder smoke. In 1612 John Rolfe introduced a milder English variety to the Virginia colony, and tobacco soon became the most important crop to the colonists. They quickly learned they could make a lot of money growing tobacco and exporting it to England. Colonists began to plant it in every available clearing—including the streets of Jamestown.

By 1616 about 2,500 pounds of Virginia tobacco were exported to England, despite what the king called "the black stinking fumes" that were taking over London shops. Two years later 20 times that amount, 50,000 pounds, was exported. Tobacco provided a good source of income for the colonists, and it created a sense of financial stability. It also brought out peculiar behavior. One colonist, commenting on the odd lack of cohesive village life, noted the colonists'

"Greediness after great quantities of tobacco causeth them after five or six years continually to remove and therefore neither build good homes, fence their grounds, or plant any orchards."

Tobacco became the primary agricultural crop throughout Virginia and the Chesapeake Bay area. As the industry mushroomed, so did the need for labor.

In 1619 three significant things happened. The first shipment of "tobacco wives"

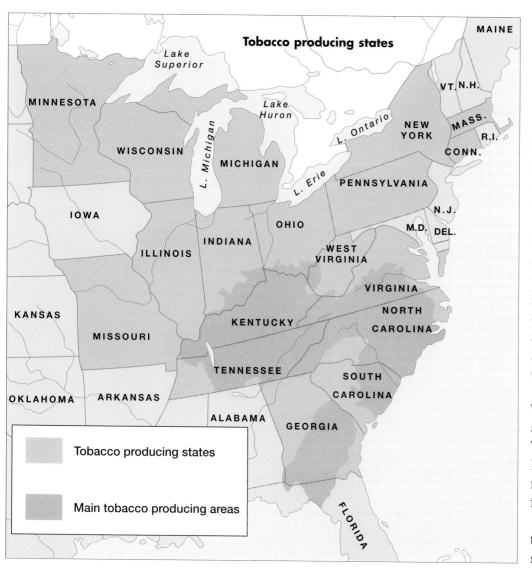

Tobacco producing states

MAINE

Lake Superior

Lake Huron

L. Ontario

L. Erie

L. Michigan

MINNESOTA

WISCONSIN

MICHIGAN

VT. N.H.

NEW YORK

MASS.

R.I.

CONN.

PENNSYLVANIA

N.J.

M.D. DEL.

IOWA

ILLINOIS

INDIANA

OHIO

WEST VIRGINIA

VIRGINIA

KANSAS

MISSOURI

KENTUCKY

NORTH CAROLINA

OKLAHOMA

ARKANSAS

TENNESSEE

SOUTH CAROLINA

ALABAMA

GEORGIA

FLORIDA

Tobacco producing states

Main tobacco producing areas

arrived in Jamestown; each woman was "sold" for 120 pounds of tobacco. Young girls who thought they wanted something better than homelessness in England were among the first to arrive to become wives (and working partners) of the early planters.

Also in 1619 the first black Africans were brought to Jamestown as workers. John Rolfe wrote in his diary "About the last of August came in a dutch man of warre that sold us twenty negars." However, slavery at that time was little different than indentured servitude, and their obligation was to work for 5–7 years before being set free. Indentured servants from England—those colonists who agreed to work for varying periods of time in exchange for freedom and passage to the New World—also came.

Child workers

The third notable event in 1619 was when the Virginia Company wrote to the London Privy Council requesting orphans and other unwanted children as workers:

> "We pray your Lordship to furnish us with one hundred [children] for next spring. Our desire is that we may have them 12 years old and upward with allowance of three pounds apiece for their transportation and forty shillings apiece for their apparel. They shall be apprentices the boys till they come to twenty-one years of age the girls till like age or until they be married."

Chesapeake tobacco planters were now dependent on imported labor to work the land, setting the stage for the next 200 years of the tobacco industry. Although effective laborers, children and indentured servants pretty well stopped coming to the colonies by 1700. Instead, planters turned to the growing African slave trade for workers. Thus the tobacco industry was the first to develop a dependence on slavery—permanent, nonvoluntary labor.

During the early colonial years there were no banks in Virginia, and British coins and currency were scarce. Planters bought items from shopkeepers on credit, paying their debts when their crops were harvested and sold. With this high demand tobacco was used as money locally and as a cash crop for export to England. A cash crop—a fairly new agricultural development at that time—is one that is grown to sell for money rather than for family or personal use. Once America began producing currency, many of those notes depicted tobacco—a symbol of its importance to early Americans.

With the rapid growth of tobacco cultivation problems soon began to emerge. Large planters grew too much, creating an excess supply. Smaller and

MANUFACTURING TOBACCO

This eighteenth-century illustration, titled "Manufacturing Tobacco," shows how the leaf is cured, aired and stored in containers called hogsheads.

less scrupulous planters began to pad their harvests by grinding other types of leaves in with tobacco and even added, as one source put it, "sweepings from their floors." As a result of this "trash tobacco" the desirability of colonial tobacco dropped, and prices began to fall. By 1660 prices fell so low, many growers were barely able to survive.

The Inspection Act

In 1730, to aid the crippled tobacco market, the Virginia Inspection Act was passed to control the quality and quantity of tobacco grown in Virginia, and to ensure planters good prices. The act required all farmers to bring their tobacco to an inspection warehouse. Enforcing the legislation was a continual concern. An open letter to the House of Burgesses in the September 24, 1736, edition of the *Virginia Gazette* asked the body to make enforcing the law its top priority:

> "It may, perhaps, be thought needless in me, to entreat Persons so well disposed to go on in the Pursuit of the real Interest of their Country, but being Watchful of the due Execution of the Tobacco-Law…I must recommend it to you, as deservedly the Principal Object of your Care. And because, by the same Act, such and so many Justices in every Country, are Authorized and Impowered to hear and report all Complaints, and to visit the Warehouses, that the Rules thereby Established must not be transgressed, I must and do expect it from them."

The Inspection Act revolutionized the tobacco market and became the standard of trade. Many planters traveled the Rappahannock River, bringing their tobacco to the inspection warehouse in Fredericksburg, Virginia, to await the arrival of big ships to take it to England. Inspectors were empowered to break

open each hogshead (barrel), remove and burn any trash, and issue tobacco notes to the owner that specified the weight and type of tobacco. If the tobacco was not good enough, it could not be sent to England, and it was destroyed. George Washington's first tobacco crops in 1759 weren't acceptable for export and he was deeply in debt by 1761.

During the Revolutionary War the Chesapeake was known as the "Tobacco Coast," and the war was known to many as "The Tobacco War." Five million pounds of Virginia tobacco helped finance the Revolution by serving as collateral for a large loan Benjamin Franklin won from France. During the war tobacco exports helped the new government build credit abroad. And when the war was over, Americans turned to tobacco taxes to help repay the Revolutionary War debt.

As postwar America began to contemplate westward expansion, tobacco became an important part of those plans. In 1781 Thomas Jefferson suggested tobacco cultivation in the "western country on the Mississippi," and in 1785 Conestoga wagons left Pennsylvania for the West. The rolled tobacco leaves inside led to the term "stogies" for cigars.

By the time of the Louisiana Purchase in 1803 tobacco was no longer the most important crop, but it was still very important to Americans. The Lewis and Clark expedition of 1804–1806 took tobacco along as a gift to the Indians—

ABOVE: **Tobacco sellers, from a 1706 engraving. This customer is sniffing the tobacco for quality.**

as "life insurance." Expedition member Patrick Gass, holed up in Fort Clatsup, Oregon, wrote:

> "Among our other difficulties, we now experience the want of tobacco. We use crabtree bark as a substitute."

But it was only a few years later when the antitobacco movement began as part of the temperance (antialcohol) movement. One 1830s source mentioned that tobacco use was considered to dry out the mouth, "creating a morbid or diseased thirst" that only liquor could quench.

A Planter's Life

A planter (someone who owns or runs a plantation) cultivates and harvests tobacco, indigo, rice, or other crops on a plantation—or, more accurately, oversees the production.

The larger the plantation, the more could be grown, bringing more wealth and influence to a planter. The wealth and influence of planters of the Chesapeake Bay area—which were considerable—depended on one crop: tobacco. As Virginia grew, so did its production of tobacco.

One pious early New England visitor noted, "the lives of the planters in Maryland and Virginia are very godless and profane," speaking primarily of their inclination to skip Sunday worship. In part this was because raising "tobo"—as the planters called tobacco—was hard year-round work. Even though many planters were from higher classes in Britain, they worked very hard on their American plantations to make them successful.

If all went well, an annual cycle began on roughly the "12th day of Christmas," when a seedbed was manured, seeded, and sheltered against frost. Because of the heavy losses to disease, cold, and insects planters seeded about 10 times the number of plants they'd eventually need. Among early planters there appeared to be different opinions about the exact time for planting, as John Clayton noted in 1688:

"The Planters differ in their Judgments about the time of planting, or pitching their Crops: Some are for pitching their Crops very early, others late, without any Distinction of the nature of the Soil....In sandy Grounds they need not strive so much for early Planting, the Looseness of the Earth, and the kind natur'd Soil, yielding all that it can, easily and speedily, and Sand retaining the Heat, makes the Plants grow faster."

After planting, the tobacco plants were tended, that is, repeatedly weeded, hoed, and debugged until they had eight to 12 leaves. This usually occurred sometime during midsummer. Keeping the plants healthy was a constant battle—tobacco was susceptible to a variety of ills:

"There are various Accidents and Distempers, where unto Tobacco is liable, as the Worm, the Fly, firing to turn, as they call them, Frenchmen, and the like. I proposed several ways to kill the Worm and Fly, as by Sulphur and the like....Tobacco-seed is very small, and by consequence so is the young

Plant at first, that if gloomy Weather happen at that time, it breeds a small Fly, which consumes the Plume of the Plant."

The next step was to "top" each plant, which meant cutting the top off so it wouldn't seed. This process then led to "suckers" appearing on the plants. They were small shoots that also needed to be removed. Around September a planter would inspect his crops, test them for moisture, aroma, maturity, and color, and decide when plants should be cut.

Once cut, leaves were hung in shaded barns to dry slowly (this produced a milder smoke). When the plants were finally dried, they were packed inside barrels called hogsheads before being shipped to England. (A hogshead was a barrel about 48 inches high and 30 inches in diameter, and held about 1,000 pounds of tobacco.) Tobo couldn't be packed when it was too moist, or it would rot. If it was too dry, tobacco would crumble. This process was best completed before Christmas so the annual cycle could begin anew.

Because tobacco was so profitable, many planters raised nothing but tobacco. This resulted in two things:

First, these planters were forced to buy their produce from other farmers. Second, tobacco quickly exhausted soil. Thus planters either had to find ways to fertilize their soil (they didn't yet know much about crop rotation) or clear more soil. It was easier and cheaper for most planters to simply keep clearing more land, with little concern for future generations. The natural byproduct of this was waste and greed, as well as the formation of very large estates that squeezed out smaller farmers. In 1688 John Clayton documented all these factors at work:

"Whereas vast Improvements might be made thereof; for the generality of Virginia is a sandy Land with a shallow soil: so that after they have clear'd a fresh piece of ground out of the Woods, it will not bear Tobacco past two or three Years, unless Cow-pened; for they manure their Ground by keeping their Cattle…but alas! they cannot improve much thus, besides it produces a strong sort of Tobacco, in which the Smoakers say they can plainly taste the fulsomness of the Dung. Therefore every three or four Years they must be for clearing a new piece of Ground out of Woods, which requires much Labour and Toil, it being so thick grown all over with massy Timber. Thus their Plantations run over vast Tracts of Ground, each ambitious of engrossing as much as they can, that they may be sure to have enough to plant, and for their Stocks and Herds of Cattle to range and to feed in; that Plantations of 1000, 2000, or 3000 Acres are common."

ABOVE LEFT: **An early American tobacco plantation, with planters in the foreground.**

RIGHT: **A domesticated tobacco plant.**

BELOW: **The beautiful 1723 Shirley House is Virginia's oldest plantation, dating back to 1613.**

Milling was the vital process to convert grain into flour. Without some form of mechanism to grind grain, the process of milling by hand (with a crude stone or wood "quern") was extremely hard and slow work.

Colonists who ground their corn "in primitive mortars, hollowed from a block of wood or the stump of a tree" used a pestle, or grinder, which was also wood, "fastened to the top of a slender sapling," which helped lift it after each blow. Thus it's easy to see that a miller—the person who owned and operated the mill—was an extremely important member of the colonial community, and his presence generally meant the difference between a meager or prosperous existence. Communities frequently offered a miller the actual mill site (on a fast-moving stream) and another choice building lot as well, promising him a local monopoly and an average of "10 percent to 15 percent of every bushel ground."

Despite a miller's importance, community members were suspicious of these high-profit individuals, and the general attitude that "no miller goes to heaven" was prevalent. Children were taught that if they found a miller "with a tuft of hair growing on his palm," they'd found an honest miller.

Some planters with large landholdings found that it was more profitable to own their own mill rather than pay a miller to grind their harvested grains. Eighteenth-century Virginia planter Landon Carter owned his own mill, but he'd been having trouble with the machinery and dam. He was forced to use the expensive services of another miller. He complained:

"The want of a mill cannot have been less loss to me than even £100 this year. My people have suffered by getting meal. No creatures could be fen through the prodigious expence of Corn more than Meal and, what is a shame to think of, no mill that I have ground at has really allowed me above one half of the meal that my grain ever made at my own mill."

The basic process of milling, as described by one early writer, involved:

"Storing grain in a hopper, feeding it between two stones [one stationary and one rotating] and sifting and sorting flour through shaker screens into collection bags."

LEFT: **A water mill at Philipsburg Manor, a preserved Dutch-American farm from the eighteenth century. The manor is located in the Hudson River Valley, North Tarrytown, New York.**

BELOW LEFT: **This 1626 Dutch engraving, known as "Hartgers View," is the earliest-known illustration of New York City. The engraving shows a windmill, ships, and American Indians in canoes near a fortified port.**

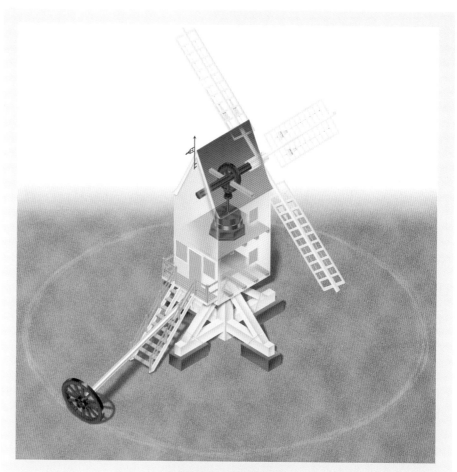

THE FIRST WINDMILL

This cutaway illustration shows the inner workings of a colonial postmill very much like Robertson's postmill, the first one in America. Pivoting on the massive main post (hidden from external view) was the crown tree. Attached to this beam was the cabin, which held the outside sails and housed the interior grinding mechanisms. Most colonial postmills were similar but varied somewhat—usually in the construction of their foundations. The wheel on the illustrated mill allowed the cabin to rotate and catch wind more effectively.

Although the process described sounds simple, accurately cut stones were needed, as was a proper balance of feed and stone spacing to keep from either burning the grain or grinding it too coarsely.

Early mills utilized water power, but colonists also knew that milling was done in Europe with windmills, making the process much easier. Indians were awed by early windmills. William Wood described their reaction in 1634.

"They" [the Indians] do much extoll & wonder at the English for their strange Inventions, especially for a Wind mill, which in their exteeme was little less than the world's wonder for the strange-ness of his whisking motion, and the sharpe teeth biting the corne (as they terme it) into such small pieces; they were loathe at the first to come neere to his long arms, or to abide in so tottering a structure."

America's first windmill

America's first windmill was erected in Watertown, Massachusetts, sometime before 1632, when it was moved to Copp's Hill in Boston for better wind. Another was constructed on Windmill Point in 1636, and three more were erected by 1650. On July 31, 1643, Henry Simons, John Button, and others were given handsome land grants on the condition that they erect "one or more corne mills, and maynteyne the same forever."

Perhaps the most familiar colonial windmill was created by William Robertson, of Williamsburg, Virginia. Robertson's mill was a postmill—a design that appeared in Europe during the Middle Ages. Its superstructure was balanced on a huge, single timber—or post—that was turned into the wind by a man at the tailpole.

The operation of a windmill was difficult work that required the miller's constant attention, but the process is fairly simple to understand. As the wind spun the blades, a shaft met a geared wheel called a "rack." The rack drove a perpendicular wooden cage gear called a pinion, which in turn moved a shaft that spun a millstone against a fixed-bed stone. Wheat and corn were steadily fed through a hopper between the stones and emerged as flour and meal.

Keeping everything running smoothly (the running stone had to turn about 110 times a minute) was difficult and dangerous, and a miller was always at the mercy of the weather. For his skill and trouble the miller traditionally received one-sixth of the grain he ground. A legislative act in 1705 set the grinding fee at one-sixth of the corn or one-eighth of the wheat.

FURS AND PELTS

> **The Restoration gallant wore his high-crowned beaver with an air, as did his lady; and he was even prepared to buy a beaver secondhand, to borrow an unbecoming hat so as to save his beaver from the rain, or to purloin his friend's beaver and leave a cheap hat in exchange.**

By the midseventeenth century a beaver felt hat was clearly a status symbol, according to this quote from a history of the Hudson Bay Company.

The use of furs and pelts in garments became fashionable in Europe as an upper-class statement, adapted from the Russians. Thanks to European deforestation furs became an upper-class commodity because fur-bearing animals (which rely on forests for survival) had become scarce by the early seventeenth century.

The forests throughout colonial America, on the other hand, were alive with fox, beaver, otter, mink, and other furbearers. Early colonists engaged in extensive fur trade with the Indians. In fact, the first shipment to England from the Pilgrims included many pelts. Over time money brought in from the fur trade bought their freedom from their merchant backers.

Of the colonies the Dutch in New York were the heaviest exporters, followed by the Chesapeake Bay area and Pennsylvania. In the Hudson Valley the Dutch were extensively involved with the fur trade from the beginning. Henry Hudson, exploring the North American coast for the Dutch East India Company, traded furs with Native Americans in 1610 at what would become New York Harbor. Robert Juet, an officer on Hudson's ship, describes meeting with the natives:

> "In the after-noone our Masters Mate went on land with an old Savage, a Govenour of the Countrey; who carried him to his house, and made him good cheere....The people of the Countrie came flocking aboord, and brought us Grapes and Pompions, which wee bought for trifles. And many brought us Bevers skinnes, and Otters skinnes, which wee bought for Beades, Knives, and Hatchets."

LEFT: **A European and an American Indian trade in beaver pelts while a second European (leaning on barrel) looks on.**

LEFT: **Andrew Jackson, fourth president of the United States, seen wearing a beaver hat.**

The Dutch used their outposts more as trading posts than colonies. In 1656 Fort Orange (Albany, New York) exported 35,000 beaver and otter skins. Even after the English took control in 1664, the trade continued to flourish, with an average of 40,000 skins exported to England annually.

Overproduction and decline

By 1699, however, the fur trade was declining—due in part to indiscriminate hunting practices, and in part because furs had now become available to the common man, making them less appealing to the wealthy. By 1704 overproduction of furs reached a point at which prices dropped sharply, and furs rotted at trading posts, waiting for a market.

In the privately owned colonies of North Carolina and South Carolina (then known as Albermarle and Clarendon), as well as in Georgia, early colonists depended on the fur trade to survive. Overtrapping had already taken its toll in the North, but this area was still virtually untapped. Colonists were able to obtain large quantities of quality furs from the Westo, Yamasee and Creek, and Coctoaw tribes of Native Americans.

Trading with the natives was profitable, but it was an unpredictable business. John Lawson, a prominent early North Carolina adventurer and entrepreneur, traded furs for about a decade. But in that role he was also the subject of multiple lawsuits for not delivering promised goods. In 1708 London merchant Micajah Perry sued Lawson, as noted in court records:

"The Defendant stands justly Indebted to the plaintiff in the Quallification aforesaid in the full and just Summe of Twelve pounds Nine Shillings and Nine pence in Merchantable Skins and furrs.

"…These are in her Majestyes name to will and require you to Arrest the body of Jno. Lawson and him Safely hold Soe that he be and appeare at the next Generall Court to be holden at the house of Captain Jno. Hecklefield in Litle river."

These minor problems aside, fur trading boomed in the South. In 1736 Augusta, Georgia, was laid out and almost immediately became one of the most important fur-trade centers in America. Pack trains brought in 100,000 pounds of skins annually. The annual receipts for Charleston, South Carolina, at the time were between 25,000 and 30,000 pounds sterling per year.

Overtrapping eventually took its toll throughout the coastal areas, and trappers moved further inland. Beyond the Allegheny Mountains trappers consistently encountered the French, who had already staked their claim.

Since the fur trade was the chief source of wealth for France in the New World, this threat from the English colonists was not taken lightly. But the French were destined from the beginning to lose their foothold. While French colonists explored the lands and rivers of the North American wilderness, English settlers were building permanent settlements, giving them a much stronger and stake in the New World.

In 1763 the French lost the French and Indian War to the English. But by then the fur trade in the known areas of North America was declining. Only the unexplored frontier offered the promise and lure of bygone glory days.

BELOW: **A Fort Bridger, Wyoming, staff member dresses in early 1800s-era clothing and demonstrates stretching a hide —one of the activities of a trapper— during a living history program. He stretches the hide over a fire to dry.**

Of the various industries that colonial Americans were involved with, the two that most positively and negatively affected the southern colonies were the successful and widespread cultivation of rice and cotton.

ABOVE: **Slaves perform duties, including baling and removing seeds, at a cotton plantation in the West Indies in this 1800 illustration.**

TOP: **Detail from a Merrimack Manufacturing cloth label (see page 27).**

Along the coasts of the Carolinas and Georgia, and along the many river mouths in those colonies there were vast acres of marshlands. Once drained and cleared of trees, these areas were well suited to growing rice. Rice was introduced to the Carolinas in 1693 as a gift to a South Carolina farmer (although there was one form of rice native to the area). This established the roots of a successful plantation colony, which supplanted the area's fur trade. These seeds—and the crop they produced—soon became known as "Carolina Golde."

The positive aspects of this industry were the huge profits accumulated by the planters and the rapid growth of colonial economy. The overwhelming negative was the dependence that was developed on the use of slave labor. In 1750 German traveler Johann Bolzius wrote home describing how African slaves—he called them "negroes"—cleared land and planted it with rice:

"If one wants to establish a plantation on previously uncultivated land, one orders the Negroes to clear a piece of land of trees and bushes first of all....The land which is to be cultivated must

be fenced with split poles 12 to 13 feet long and nearly 4 inches thick. Every Negro must split 100 of such poles per day from oaks or firs....In the evening all the Negroes must occupy themselves with burning the cut bushes and the branches."

The letter went on to describe a difficult, year-long schedule of tasks for growing rice—all done by "negroes." Colonial planters had little or no experience with the crop and relied heavily on the efforts of blacks who knew of rice cultivation from their native Africa. As a result planting and cultivation methods developed in South Carolina closely resembled those used in Africa. By 1726

BELOW: **An early illustration of a rice field shows the cycle of work. The center shows dozens of slave laborers with several overseers. At left and right of the vignette are shown specific jobs, including ditching and reaping.**

"Carolina Golde" was the world standard for the best rice available, and rice was one of the few things the colonists were allowed to freely export. This success stimulated more rice cultivation, which was highly labor intensive, and required even more slaves being imported from Africa. In 1735 Samuel Eveleigh of Charleston wrote:

"I am positive that the Commodity can't be produced by white people. Because the work is too laborious, the heat very intent, and the whites can't work in the wett at that season as Negrs do to weed rice."

Rice seeds were sown in late spring and required hand weeding and care until the fall. In early September slaves with sickles cut rice stalks and bound them in sheaves. They were then stacked for curing. Slaves then had to thresh the stalks by hand and winnow the chaff before barreling up the rice for export. Production of rice advanced at an ever-accelerating rate.

By 1730 Parliament permitted the exportation of rice to any port south of Cape Finistere, which in turn saved the rice planter from British duties and allowed him to pocket the middleman's profit. With these restrictions dropped, the rice industry exploded. Between 1724 and 1736 alone the export rate of rice nearly tripled from 19,908 to 53,376 barrels. As the rice industry rose, so also did the slave population. The two seemed to perpetuate each other: The expansion of rice cultivation demanded more slave labor, which in turn allowed greater expansion of the plantations.

During the mid-1740s an extended conflict with the Spanish crippled South Carolina's economy. A Spanish naval blockade prevented rice crops from reaching the West Indies. This led to the introduction of indigo, used to make a red-purple dye for textiles, which became another huge source of wealth for the South. The growth of indigo also permanently crippled the rice industry, which saw significant decreases in export from 1770 to 1790.

Deteriorating relations with Great Britain also affected the money flow created by these profitable crops. Something had to be done.

The invention of the cotton gin

Although we frequently think of cotton farming when we think about farming in the South, cotton was grown primarily for home use only until the late eighteenth century. It was simply too difficult to extract the seeds from the useful fibers to make it commercially successful on any large scale: "a worker could remove seeds from only about one pound of cotton per day." As late as 1791 West Indian cotton was preferred to its American counterpart because it was cleaner. Moses Brown, writing in that same year, made the observation that:

"The present production in the mixed manner in which it [American cotton] is Brought to Market does not answer good purpose."

As a result, cotton did not become an important commercial crop until three situations converged during the 1790s.

First, there were the previously mentioned problems with the rice and indigo markets that forced planters to consider a change. Then in 1790 Samuel Slater opened the first textile mill in Pawtucket, Rhode Island, increasing the demand for cotton.

Then just three years later, in 1793, Eli Whitney invented the cotton gin (engine) in an unlikely turn of events. Whitney, a young man who had recently graduated from Yale, traveled south to begin work as a tutor for children in South Carolina. He first traveled to Georgia, where he "heard much said of the extreme difficulty of ginning Cotton, that is separating it from its seeds." He wrote his father that:

"If a machine could be invented which would clean the cotton with

expedition, it would be a great thing both the Country and the inventor. I involuntarily happened to be thinking on the subject and struck out a plan of a Machine in my mind."

Within a short period of time young Whitney had developed a prototype of the machine, for which he was offered a substantial sum. Rather than continue on to South Carolina, Whitney wrote, he elected to stay in Georgia to work on his invention:

"I concluded to relinquish my school and turn my attention to perfecting the Machine. I made one

BELOW: **This illustration shows slaves picking cotton on a plantation. Such work was very hot, uncomfortable, and bloody, as pickers were injured by the husks surrounding the cotton.**

before I came away which required the labor of one man to turn it and with which one man will clean ten times as much cotton as he can in any other way before known and also cleanse it much better than in the usual mode. This machine may be turned by water or with a horse, with the greatest ease, and one man and a horse will do more than fifty men with the old machines. It makes the labor fifty times less, without throwing any class of People out of business."

The end result, the ingeniously simple cotton gin, was functional by April 1793. The cotton gin was described as:

"A roller with hooks turned by hand. The hooks pull cotton through slots too small for the seeds, then a roller passes over a rotating brush carrying pure fiber to bottom of the machine."

The growth of cotton culture

Although he applied for (and received) a patent, Whitney was unable to protect his rights from imitators, and similar devices soon appeared. Production of cotton went from one pound to 50 pounds of cotton per worker per day. Demand from textiles mills soon exploded, bringing about another financial boom for a crop that depended extensively on a self-perpetuating need for slave labor—despite movements in the North to abolish the practice.

After the War of 1812 the crushing new demand for cotton led many small and midsize planters to turn to cotton and become (if they weren't already) slave owners. Cotton culture swept through the southern states, creating a single-crop market that relied on slave labor—a fact that would come to haunt them soon enough.

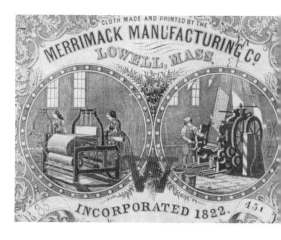

ABOVE: **A cloth label identifying Merrimack Manufacturing in Lowell, Massachusetts. It was this manufacturer that revolutionized the textile industry.**

BELOW: **A male and female slave work a cotton gin, removing seeds and sacking the cotton. Although this was hard work, the gin (engine) allowed a single worker to increase his or her daily production by nearly 50 times.**

The Colonial Gentry

Typically there are no higher classes without one group unfairly taking advantage of the efforts of some other group. There was no "high-born society" in colonial America to speak of. But the rise of the colonial gentry was swift, due in large part to the efforts of others—namely slaves.

The colonial gentry was composed primarily of large tobacco, rice, indigo, and—later—cotton planters. A small number of large estates controlled a large percentage of colonial wealth, owned numerous slaves, and set the social standards that controlled the political affairs of much of the South. There were, however, somewhat different attitudes between the wealthy of the North and South. The daughter of a Virginia tobacco farmer who became a Mississippi cotton farmer noted:

"The plainer classes in Virginia, like those in England, from whom they were descended, recognized the difference between themselves and the higher classes, and did not aspire to social equality. But in Mississippi the tone was different. They resented anything like superiority in breeding."

The lifestyle of the colonial gentry changed somewhat over the years. Early references about early rice plantations speak of masters "laboring side-by-side with slaves." By the eighteenth century much of gentry life was spent in the pursuit of idle pleasures.

Numerous private clubs sprang up across the countryside where, according to one northern visitor to Charles Town (Charleston, South Carolina), "cards, dice, the bottle and horses engross prodigious portions of time and attention." All conversation eventually turned to "land, negroes, and rice." Others frequented their hunting clubs where afternoons were "spent very merry, after killing foxes."

While much of this merriment was limited to male owners, there were large social occasions for all members of the gentry to mingle. Eliza Wilkinson, writing in the 1760s, described preparations for a ball:

"The important day arrived, and there was such powdering! and frizzing and curling! and dressing."

One at the ball, Wilkinson found that:

"The Muzík played sweetly, so sweetly that I could not keep my feet still."

As today, estates were bought and sold. The real-estate ads in colonial Charleston were fascinating. One Charleston estate,

LEFT: Ballroom in Richmond, Virginia. Such lavish surroundings were not uncommon to the colonial gentry.

BELOW LEFT: If you were rich enough, a sedan chair was a useful method of transportation.

BELOW RIGHT: A lace tablecloth adorns a table in a small dining room in Carter's Grove Plantation, a mansion in Colonial Williamsburg decorated in the colonial revival style. The most wealthy of the colonists demanded the finest surroundings and creature comforts.

advertised for sale in 1765, included:

"A large two-story Mansion House" facing the river, an overseer's house and slave cabins, with "land sufficient to work 50 or 60 Negroes on corn, rice, and indigo for one hundred years."

Another 400-acre estate for sale at the same time included "upward of fifty likely strong negroes."

Charles Town was arguably the hub of gentry life. During the winter of 1773–1774 a total of 77 different plays were performed at one new structure in particular. On opening night all things, including the sets, costumes, and music, were perfect, according to the *New York Gazette*. The paper gushed about the theater:

"It is elegantly furnished…the most commodious on the continent.…The "disposition of the lights contributed to the satisfaction of the audience who expressed the highest approbation of their entertainment."

But the class of the new rich was not without its critics. Dr. Alexander Garden of Charleston had the following to say about

the lifestyles of the rich. He felt they were:

"Absolutely above every occupation but eating, drinking, lolling, smoking, and sleeping which five modes constitute the essence of their life and existence."

This was an existence that eventually led to a serious alcohol dependency problem in this part of the new country.

Another northern visitor observed that "the rich [are] haughty and insolent," and went on to characterize these traits as springing from a life of slave ownership, which essentially trained the:

"Country gentlemen from infancy to tyrannize. They carry with them a disposition to treat all mankind in the same manner."

New England rum was one of the more interesting colonial exports. It was also instrumental to the shipbuilding, whaling, and slave trades. It played prominent roles in colonial society and, ultimately, the Revolutionary War.

George Washington campaigned with "seventy-five gallons of free rum" distributed to the voters of Virginia who elected him to the House of Burgesses in 1758. Paul Revere was said to have had two glasses of Medford (another name for rum) before his famous midnight ride.

Cheap and potent, New England rum was distilled from fermented molasses. Early on, rum (an American name) was called "Barbadoes-liquor," "Barbadoes-brandy," "strong water," or "kill-devil"; and it was known as "ocuby" (pronounced Oh-koo-bee) by the Indians as well as many white settlers. A 1651 description of Barbados is the earliest-known specific reference to rum:

> "The chief fudling they make in the island is Rumbullion, alias Kill-Devil, and this is made of sugar canes distilled, a hot, hellish, and terrible liquor."

A description of Surinam, also written in 1651, says "Rhum made from sugar-canes is called kill-devil in New England," indicating the very early association with the colonies.

The New York Dutch soon called all liquor "New England rum." The May 1657 Act of the General Court of Massachusetts prohibited the sale of strong liquors using, as the Dutch did, "rum" as slang for other types of alcohol "whether knowne by the name of rumme, strong water, wine, brandy."

The distilling industry grew steadily. In 1673 rum imported from Barbados sold cheaply for about 6 schillings per gallon. By 1687 its price had plummeted, and New England rum (made in the colonies from Indies molasses) sold for 1 schilling, 6 pence per gallon—less than a third of the import's former price. Indies molasses was cheaper still, and production and demand increased.

New England rum was, indeed, cheap enough. Puritan parson Reverend Increase Mather wrote in 1686:

> "It is an unhappy thing that in later years a Kind of Drink called Rum has been common among us. They that are poor and wicked, too, can for a penny make themselves drunk."

Another colonist said:

> "My dear countrymen are fonder of it than they are of their wives and children, for they often sell the bread out of their mouths to buy rum to put in their own."

Rum became the most popular drink in the colonies, and many common people considered it as necessary as flour.

Baron Friedrich Adolf von Riedesel, who commanded Brunswick troops in America during the Revolution, wrote of New England inhabitants: "Most of the males have a strong passion for strong drink, especially rum," and John Adams said, "If the ancients drank wine as our people drink rum and cider, it is no wonder we hear of so many possessed with devils."

The whites weren't the only ones fond of rum. It was extensively traded with the Indians. William Penn wrote to the Earl of Sutherland in 1683:

> "Ye Dutch, Sweed, and English have by Brandy and Specially Rum, almost Debaucht ye Indians all. When Drunk ye most Wretched of Spectacles."

Numerous court records exist referring to laws restraining the sale of rum to the "bloudy salvages."

A profitable export

Regardless, New England rum and its production remained an important part of colonial life and a hugely profitable export. It also became "indispensible to

LEFT: ***Overindulgence of Alcohol***—an 1820 woodcut cartoon—was intended to show the afflictions blamed on drinking too much, including fever, cholera, murder, epilepsy, and others.

BELOW: **A 1763 illustration of a cognac distillery shows some of the stages in the process.**

the fishing fleets, Indian trade, and slaving business," primarily as a trading tool. Casks stood in every country store and tavern, and rum was the basis of all popular tavern drinks such as the "toddy, sling, grog," and others.

By the mid-1700s, largely because of the tremendously unpopular (but largely unenforced) 1733 Molasses Act, colonial sugar and molasses refineries grew to total 26. The Molasses Act was designed to protect British West Indies planters by placing heavy taxes on non-British sugar. Of the approximately 8.5 million gallons distilled per year from imported molasses in the mid-1700s, 60 percent was consumed by colonists. Around 1750 one traveler noted:

> "The quantity of spirits which they distill in Boston from the molasses which they import is as surprising as the cheapness at which they sell it, which is under two shillings a gallon; but they are more famous for the quantity and cheapness than for the excellency of their rum."

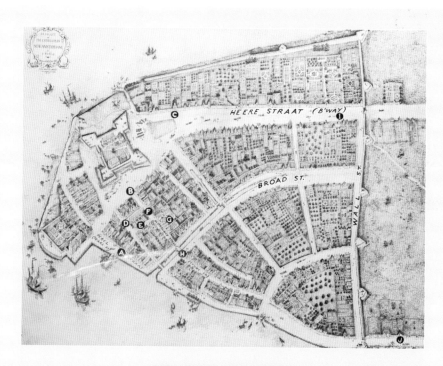

NEW YORK BREWERIES

This map of southern Manhattan Island shows how many breweries New York City already had by 1660. The key identifies: A: warehouse built by Governor William Kieft in 1641, which included the first tavern; B: brewery of Jaonnes Couwenhoven; C: Martin Creiger's tavern; D: West India Company's brewery and warehouse; E: Jacop Kip's brewery; F: brewery of Isaac de Foreest sold to Harman Rutgers in 1693; G: Oloff van Cortlandt's brewhouse, behind his home on Brouwer (Brewers') Straat, now Stone Street; H: Jacob von Couwenhoven's brewery; I: brewery of Isaac Van Vleck bought from Pieter Wolfertson van Couwenhoven; J: brewery outside city wall bought from Thomas Hall by William Beekman. As this old map shows, even the streets were "wet"; the old canal ran almost the full length of Broad Street.

In 1764 the Molasses Act was replaced by the Sugar Act, which provided for slightly lower taxes on molasses but increased duties on refined sugar, coffee, wine, and other non-British products to pay for British soldiers quartered in the colonies.

By 1774 there were 63 rum distilleries in Massachusetts alone, producing 2.7 million gallons per year. As the British tightened their pre-Revolution grip by setting up naval blockades, it became difficult to import molasses and export rum, leading to the first decline in demand in nearly 150 years. Whiskey, including rye and bourbon, became the liquor of choice for many, and just as profitable.

After the Revolutionary War rum production was still an important industry but continued a slow decline that didn't change until after the blockades of the War of 1812.

> **Lake Superior**
> Lake Huron
> L. Michigan
> L. Ontario
> L. Erie
> VT. N.H.
> NEW YORK
> MASS.
> R.I.
> CONN.
> PENNSYLVANIA
> N.J.
> M.D. DEL.
> WEST VIRGINIA
> VIRGINIA
> KENTUCKY
> NORTH CAROLINA
> SOUTH CAROLINA
> GEORGIA
> FLORIDA

Flax
Cereals
Fruit
Indigo
Rice
Tobacco
Cotton

Colonial cash crop growing ranges

❝Those who labor in the earth are the chosen people of God, if ever He had a chosen people, whose breasts He has made His peculiar deposit for genuine and substantial virtue.❞

Thomas Jefferson thought very highly of people who devoted their lives to agriculture—but his view of the colonial farmer wasn't shared by all. A seventeenth-century Virginian called them those:

"Who sponge upon the blessings of a warm sun and fruitful soil, and almost grutch [grudge] the pains of gathering in the bounties of the earth."

Despite these widely varying opinions of our earliest agriculturists, much has been written about how the American colonist essentially invented the farm as we now know it—the semi-isolated, self-sufficient parcel of land. Such units existed previously in Scotland and in some parts of England, but were not common. The dense population in Britain meant most life revolved around the village, where merchants, craftsmen, churches, and pubs were easily accessible. But it was in America that farmers found the land, streams, and shorelines necessary for a self-sufficient lifestyle.

Once established, this new style of farming affected all aspects of colonial agriculture. It was so pervasive that even as late as 1760, 90 percent of all Americans derived their livelihood from the soil.

The earliest colonial farmers simply used what land had been previously cleared by Indians before setting out to clear more. In 1619 John Rolfe wrote:

"An industrious man not otherwise employed may well tend four acres of corn and 1,000 plants of tobacco; and where they say and acre will yield three or four barrels, we have ordinarily four or five, but of

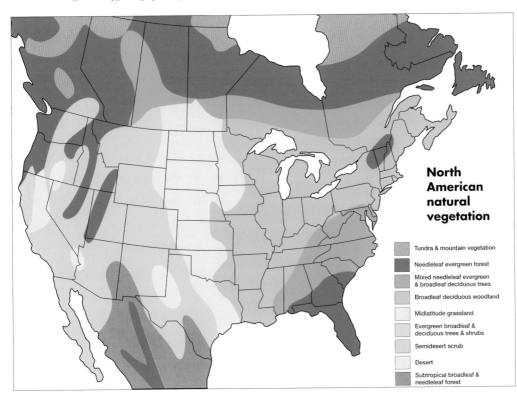

North American natural vegetation

Tundra & mountain vegetation
Needleleaf evergreen forest
Mixed needleleaf evergreen & broadleaf deciduous trees
Broadleaf deciduous woodland
Midlatitude grassland
Evergreen broadleaf & deciduous trees & shrubs
Semidesert scrub
Desert
Subtropical broadleaf & needleleaf forest

LEFT: **The map at left shows colonial America cash crop distribution, each coded by color to indicate its growing range.**

BELOW LEFT: **North American natural vegetation distribution is shown by the color-coded map. Climate, soil types, and natural vegetation have a lot to do with what types of crops can be grown in an area.**

new ground six, seven, and eight… so that one man can provide corn for five, and apparel for two, by the profit of his tobacco."

The first settlers, finding that European agriculture could not easily be transferred to the new environment, adopted the Indian practice of raising corn, squash, tobacco, and other crops. Corn was, from the beginning, the leading food crop and was grown in all the colonies. Tobacco, which was exported for money, was raised mostly in Virginia and Maryland. Many of those farmers chose to raise exclusively tobacco, buying their food from other colonists.

It is hard for us to imagine, but much of the Eastern Seaboard consisted of dense forest; ground that had never been "broken." As colonists moved inland, they faced the exceedingly difficult task of "clearing the land," coining a phrase that has stayed in our language to denote hard work. It is estimated a settler could expect to clear no more than perhaps two acres per year, girdling trees (cutting a broad band of bark around the tree to kill it), cutting down trees, clearing brush, and removing rocks (stumps were simply left to decay). If extremely lucky, such a farmer would have maybe 80-100 acres to pass to a son at the end of his productive life—although brush, rocks, and other trash were generally left on land that became "used up."

Early colonial farmers used crude hand tools made entirely of wood, some-times (but rarely) with iron parts. Their main tools included the shovel, hoe, and mattock (a digging tool resembling a cross between a pick and a hoe). Plows were very rare until the 1670s. Planting, weeding, and harvesting were all done by hand, keeping farmers perpetually in a pattern of "garden husbandry," as opposed to "field husbandry."

In addition to the staple food of corn, gardens frequently contained peas, cabbage, carrots, parsnips, turnips, and onions. Tomatoes weren't cultivated because they were believed to be poisonous by the colonists. Orchards were usually planted nearby, mostly with apple and peach trees. The orchards supplied nutritious fruit that was often made into alcoholic beverages such as brandy, cider, and applejack.

In New England farmers on small acreages raised corn, oats, rye, vegetables, fruits, and livestock (cattle and sheep). In the central colonies of New York, Pennsylvania, and New Jersey wheat was the major crop. Farmers in this region also produced livestock, as well as fruit and vegetables. Southern colonies became the primary producers of nonfood crops such as tobacco, indigo, and cotton, although they did raise a lot of rice as well.

As has always been the case, colonial farmers were dependent on weather and were always at the mercy of nature. Although these early farmers accepted these unpredictable forces, there were many extremes of American weather and nature they had not foreseen: Hurricanes, years-long droughts, tobacco flies, raccoons, and even the now-extinct passenger pigeon. The latter were known as "maize thiefs"; they could flatten an entire crop when huge migrating flocks landed in fields around harvest time.

The technological advances of the early nineteenth century began to bring about changes that transformed American agriculture from small-scale family farming to much larger operations.

CORN

Corn was an agricultural miracle to the colonists. It was good for humans and livestock, it was easy to grow with little tending, it produced well, and it was resistant to many diseases. Corn could be served fresh or dried. Dried corn could be either rehydrated or ground and used for other purposes. Aside from the food value, corn served many other functions: Stalks were used as winter food for livestock, husks were used to stuff mattresses, and cobs were used as jug stoppers, tool handles, and as bowls for pipes.

Indians taught the settlers to plant corn "when the white oak leaves reach the size of a mouse's ear." Throughout the colonies corn season consisted of:

"Men and women moving through the mire, bending over about six thousand times a day, making holes in the crowns of hills 'with their fingers or a small stick' for the reception of the corn seeds."

They dropped three to four kernels in holes about three to four feet apart, "mounding or hilling" the seedlings once they sprouted. Corn was then fertilized by burying fish in the mounds—great schools of shad that swam up streams each spring to spawn and die. To keep dogs from digging up rotting fish, farmers tied "one forepaw to the neck for forty days after planting."

The Indians further taught the settlers the "three sisters" system of planting. When the corn stalks were two or three feet high, beans and pumpkin seeds were planted around them. The beans climbed the corn stalks for support, and the pumpkin plants served as ground cover, discouraging weed growth. The bean-laden corn stalks provided shade for the pumpkins.

The colonists in many ways (certainly the Pilgrims more than the Jamestown colonists) truly were greeted by a natural paradise. The variety and quantity of usable flora and fauna were nothing short of awesome.

According to William Bradford, in the spring:

> "Herrings come up in such abundance into their brooks and fords to spawn that it is almost impossible to ride through without treading on them."

Huge flocks of hundreds of turkeys and tens of thousands of ducks were common. In fact, according to Bradford, the ducks were so plentiful that they blotted out the sun when they rose from a pond and made "a rushing and vibration of the air like a great storm coming through the trees."

Nonetheless it was difficult for early colonists to easily take advantage of the abundant resources they found. Most had never used a gun of any sort, and the months-long journey across the ocean drained them mightily. Captain John Smith made the comment that:

> "Though there be fish in the sea, fowls in the air, and beasts in the woods, their bounds are so large,

ABOVE: **Shown here is a man whaling with a harpoon gun. These devices, which made killing whales easier, were invented during the eighteenth century but were highly dangerous to the whalers as well.**

ABOVE RIGHT: **Hunting was plentiful in the New World—particularly birds of the turkey family, as illustrated here: clockwise; the American wild turkey, galeated curassow, red curassow, crested curassow.**

BELOW LEFT: **A 1665 engraving titled "Beached Whale and Other Sea Life" shows the public spectacle created by such an event. Early American colonists relied more on beached whales than those they killed themselves.**

> they so wild, and we so weak and ignorant, we cannot much trouble them."

Early colonists knew little about hunting, and any meat they consumed was generally from domesticated animals. Over time, at least for the more common people, this changed. Hunting was a good way to supplement the food supplies of colonial families, but it rarely

generated much income—unless the colonists were hunting animals with desirable furs and pelts. Hunting also became a popular hobby—much as it is now. Robert Beverley's account of late seventeenth-century New England mentions recreational "hunting, fishing, and fowling, with which they entertain themselves an hundred ways." This type of hunting provided a much-needed break for the colonists. Another account of recreational hunting describes the process that took place after driving a hapless rabbit up a hollow tree:

"The business is to kindle a fire, and smother them with smoke, till they let go their hold and fall to the bottom stifled, from whence they take them. If they have a mind to spare their lives, upon turning them loose they will be as fit as ever to hunt another time, for the mischief done them by the smoke immediately wears off."

These rabbit hunts were no doubt the colonial equivalent of the modern British fox hunt.

Robert Beverley's account of "vermin" hunting (raccoon and opossum) tells a similar tale of entertainment:

"It is perform'd afoot with small dogs in the night by the light of the moon or stars. Wherever the dog barks, you may depend upon finding the game, and this alarm draws men and dogs that way."

Once the unfortunate quarry was treed:

"They detach a nimble fellow up after it, who must have a scuffle with the beast before he can throw it down to the dogs, and then the sport increases to see the vermin encounter those little curs."

Young men also enjoyed hunting for wild horses, which were, according to Berkeley, "foaled in the woods of the uplands that never were in hand and are as shy as any savage creature." These wild horses were so swift they were extremely difficult to capture unless injured, old, or lame. So for most of the young men this activity was about the thrill of the chase. Even if captured healthy, many of the wild horses were "so sullen they can't be tam'd."

The fishing industry

Fishing, on the other hand, became a profitable enterprise in New England early on and stayed that way. The waters off the coast of New England have been the source of livelihood since the earliest settlements—and earlier. Even during

the sixteenth century Dutch, Portugese, English, and French navigators fished the cold north Atlantic waters, exploiting the rich supply of fish, which was the primary flesh food of Europeans.

In 1590 Sir Walter Raleigh declared the American fisheries as the "stay and support of the west counties of England." Within a few years after the settlement of Jamestown Captain John Smith extolled the virtues of fish:

"Let not the meaness of the word Fish distaste you, for it will afford as good gold as the mines of Guiana and Potassie with less hazard of charge, and more certainty and facility."

By 1633 Boston began exporting fish, and soon almost every port had a fishing fleet, bringing in supplies of cod, mackerel, halibut, bass, herring, sturgeon,

hake, and other deep-sea fish. To encourage this industry, in 1639 the Massachusetts general court exempted for seven years fishing vessels and other property associated with the industry from all duties and public taxes. In addition, fishermen and shipbuilders were exempt from military service.

Probably the most important type of fish to the colonists was the cod. It served as an inexhaustible supply of food for the colonies and for exporting to Europe. It also had been considered a sacred fish, symbolizing the blessing that Providence bestowed on those who walked the path of righteousness. Each take of cod was divided into three grades. The best grade, or "merchantable," was dried and salted. It brought good prices in European Catholic communities. Midgrade fish was consumed fresh in the colonies, often being the staple food during winter

months. The lowest grade of cod, designated as "refuse," was shipped to the West Indies and sold as food for slaves.

Somewhat related to New England's fishing is the whaling industry, which began as early as 1614. Captain John Smith visited the New England coast that year "to take whales and make trials at a mine of gold and copper." By 1622, when *Brief Relation of the Discovery and Plantation of New England* was published, a rich source of whales was already being promoted:

"Whales of the best kind for oil and bone are said to abound near Cape Cod which for that reason is spoken of as likely to be a place of good fishing."

In 1635 Richard Mather wrote about:

"Mighty whales spewing water in the air like the smoke of a

chimney…of such incredible bigness that I will never wonder that the body of Jonah could be in the belly of a whale."

Whales were wrongly assumed by most people to be fish, and whaling was thought to be important for two reasons. First, whales were the source of many usable products, including blubber, oil, and bone. Second, people incorrectly thought that killing whales helped preserve the fish supply for humans. The Reverend J.G. Wood described the sperm whales "destructive among lesser fishes…and can at one gulp swallow a shoal of fishes down its enormous gullet." His description of the whaling process rang with pride:

"With…few and simple weapons, the fishers contrive to secure the monster of the waters—a beautiful instance of the superiority of

reason over brute strength. The whale-fisher…achieves a task which may be compared to a mouse attacking and killing a wolf with a reel of thread and a crochet needle."

The earliest colonial whalers had to rely on those whales that beached themselves, but they soon learned how to harpoon whales from small boats. The earliest whale to be commercially exploited was the so-called "right whale," a name that stuck. The right whale got its name because early whalers said it was "the right whale to hunt." Why? Because these slow-moving whales stayed close to shore, were peaceful, and they floated when dead, making them easier to get to shore. Whaling soon expanded to include sperm, white, and other types of whales.

In 1715 Christopher Hussey of Nantucket Island, Massachusetts, built a vessel capable of towing sperm whales

ashore. A few years later the ability to extract oil on board was developed, allowing whalers to broaden their territory north to the Arctic Ocean and south to the coast of Brazil. By 1774 more than 360 vessels were dedicated to whaling. Of these, 120 were from Nantucket, 180 were from other ports in Massachusetts, and the remainder spread between Connecticut, Rhode Island, and New York. The Dutch were the first to organize whaling as an industry. It was founded first on Long Island and Cap Cod, later shifting to Nantucket and New Bedford, where it was centered until the decline of the industry in the 1850s.

BELOW LEFT: *Whale Fishery,* a print by Currier & Ives, shows the up-close and dangerous approach used by many American whalers

BELOW: **This 1822 painting shows a hunting camp in a pine forest.**

LIVESTOCK FARMING

Despite the importance of cattle and pork farming to our modern United States, the American colonies weren't known for their meat production. Many colonists could not afford to keep livestock, and they depended on wild game for their primary meat supply.

Venison (deer), ducks, rabbits, and many other types of game were regular parts of a colonist's diet. Most early colonists did little more than feed their own families. Nonetheless, domesticated meat animals accompanied the earliest of the voyagers. One such adventurer, Master Hamor, one of Captain John Smith's early Jamestown party, mentioned the arrival of animals:

> "Before Lord la Warr arrived in England, the Council and Company had dispatched away Sir Thomas Dale with three ships, men, and cattle, and all other provisions necessary for a year; all of which arrived well [on] the tenth of May, 1611."

In 1635 one colonist listed as his inventory "sixty-four goats, ninety-two sheep, twenty-two horses, and fifty-eight cattle." Although this particular colonist was obviously more well to do than many, he shared one thing in common with most early farmers—no fowl. Chickens were thought to be of little use until it was discovered—near the end of the seventeenth century—that they did well with a diet of dried corn kernels.

As the supply of domestic livestock increased, having been brought over from England (the Indians could offer only dog

for domesticated meat), colonists began raising livestock for commercial purposes. Pork soon became the primary meat. This is because a hog could easily forage, existing on whatever it found to eat. Also, it was far easier to use all of a hog—"all but the squeal," according to an old saying. The meat from "four good-sized hogs, salted and preserved" could carry a family through the toughest of winters. In addition, the intestines were used as sausage casings, bladders to hold lard, and the long hair to sew buckskins.

Goats found early favor with colonists because—much like hogs—they required little care. They also provided milk and cheese. But goats soon became troublesome because they destroyed gardens. Sheep were handy for their wool, but they were picky eaters, left little for other livestock, and were highly vulnerable to wolves.

Cattle, along with hogs, were highly valued early on for both food and as a cash asset. Plymouth settlers survived early problems by selling excess cattle to Massachusetts. In 1660 one settler noted:

> "It is a wonder to consider how many thousands neat beasts and hogs are yearly killed and have been for many years past for provision in

the country and sent abroad to supply Newfoundland, Barbados and Jamaica."

In the Chesapeake area cattle were considered more valuable than land—being "the most secure commodity of wealth," as one colonist put it. Because cattle were of such value, it's no surprise that there were also early cattle rustlers. This led to the colonists finding some way to mark their cattle. Early branding consisted of nicks, slits, or other forms of minor disfigurement. Wesley Frank Craven commented that ear notching was popular as:

> "A relatively insensible member of the body and of practically no utility to any other than the beast itself."

He went on to note that "Earmarks—nicks, slits, croppings, underbits, overbits, and holes"—placed on either or both ears offered an amazing number of combinations. These markings were then registered with the town clerk.

Predators such as wolves weren't the only problem for early colonial livestock farmers. Hurricanes, harsh winters (such as 1672-1673, which killed half of the unsheltered colonial cattle), and other natural problems were constants. Virginia

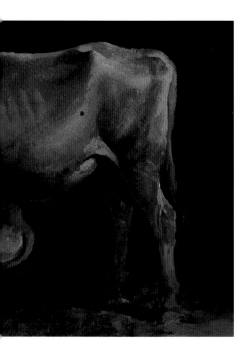

ABOVE: **Cattle were extremely valuable in the New World—"the most secure commodity of wealth."**

BELOW: **In this early caricature Andrew Resolute, Uncle Sam's faithful teamster, is shown taking the produce of the farms to another storehouse and giving Uncle Sam his reasons for doing so.**

historian Robert Beverley also questioned the animal husbandry skills of colonists in the face of these challenges:

> "When I come to speak of their cattle, I can't forbear charging my countrymen with exceeding ill husbandry, in not providing sufficiently for them all winter, by which means they starve their young cattle, or at least stint their growth; so that they seldom or never grow so large as they would do, if people can but save the lives of their cattle, though they suffer them to be never so poor in the winter, yet they will presently grow fat again in the spring, which they esteem sufficient for their purpose. And this is the occasion, that their beef and mutton are seldom or never so large, or so fat as in England. And yet with the least feeding imaginable, they are put into as good case as can be desired; and it is the same with their hogs."

Plant pests

Even plant pests caused problems for colonial livestock producers. For exam-ple, jimson weed (a name adapted from "Jamestown weed") drove cattle crazy. It didn't do much for those humans who were brave (or foolish) enough to try it, either. One settler commented that the weed turned the men into

> "Natural fools [who] would have wallowed in their own excrement if they had not been prevented."

Over time, colonists became involved in trading meat with the West Indies in exchange for molasses to distill into New England rum. Meat was salted, smoked, and packed into wooden barrels or boxes for storage and shipping—hence the term "meat packing." William Pynchon of Springfield, Massachusetts, is recorded as the first American devoted to the "packing" business. In 1655 he started by driving cattle to Boston and was packing large numbers of hogs by 1662. Colonial butchers operated the first retail meat shops. Having learned their trade in Europe, local butchers supplied meat to others in the community beyond their own immediate family as an important form of local trade.

IRON INDUSTRY

Among the earliest of true American industries was the iron industry. Although settlers brought metal tools and implements with them, they were scarce, and there was a need to be able to manufacture such goods in the New World.

Early explorers quickly identified the rich mineral potential of the new country. Thomas Hariot, working on behalf of Sir Walter Raleigh, noted in his 1585 publication *A Briefe and True Report of the New Found Land of Virginia*:

> "In two places of the country specially one about four score and the other six score miles from the fort or place where we dwelt, wee found neer the water side the ground to be rockie, which, by triall of a minerall man, was founde to hold iron richly. It is founde in manie places of the countrey else. I know nothing to the contrarie but that it maie bee allowed, for a good marchantable commoditie."

At about the same time, settlers in the lost Roanoke Colony found deposits of "bog iron" that was said to "grow in ponds." This form of native iron was extremely rich ore that was "fished out of ponds" with long-handled tongs. One New England pond in particular was said to have yielded more than 300 tons of ore per year for more than 60 years.

Although smelting was attempted early on in Virginia, it wasn't until the Puritans established a "furnace" in Lynn, Massachusetts, that the industry truly began to grow. That furnace was described as "a large fireplace," and a bigger and better one was built in Saugus in 1646. It could produce up to eight tons of iron each week that was of a quality high enough to be used for pots and wrought-iron bars. In these "furnaces" iron ore was smelted into pig iron and was later further refined.

The basic structure of these early furnaces consisted of stone towers with sloping walls on rectangular foundations. A 30-foot (or so) chimney rose from the center of the structure. Inside the structure was a roughly egg-shaped chamber in which fuel (charcoal), ore, and flux (oyster shells or limestone) could be dumped in layers from a platform. Flux helped to release the impurities from the ore. Molten iron ran from the bottom into sand molds to form "pigs." Fires were fueled by bellows powered by large water wheels.

By the 1730s England was running out of available forests to fuel its iron furnaces. Because the crown did not want to become too dependent on imports from Scandinavian countries, Parliament explored incentives to encourage iron production in the

ABOVE: **A smelting furnace, built in the 1700s, stands in the Catoctin Iron Works in Maryland. This furnace, located at Cunningham Falls State Park, Thurmont, Maryland, made munitions for General Washington's army during the American Revolution.**

RIGHT: **The American ironworks factory in Pittsburgh, Pennsylvania. Such ironworks, generally located on rivers, belched huge black clouds into American skies and dumped waste into the water.**

LEFT: **Philadelphia's Liberty Bell being tested in 1753 at the Pass and Stow Foundry, with American statesman, writer, and scientist Benjamin Franklin (1706–1790) (hat under arm) present.**

colonies. The British urged Americans to smelt as much ore into pig iron as possible but discouraged the practice of making it into any finished form. England thought of the colonies only as a source of raw materials, and that the colonies should not compete or take jobs from the mother country.

Soon the iron industry grew and spread into Connecticut, New Jersey, Pennsylvania, Maryland, and Virginia, with the hub centered in Pennsylvania after 1750. This rapid growth made British manufacturers nervous.

Restricting American industry

The Iron Act of 1750 was enacted by Parliament to slow the development of colonial manufacturing in competition with British industry. The law restricted the American iron industry to supplying raw metals. Therefore, everything that was used on a daily basis by the colonists was supposed to be "Made in England" not in the colonies. To meet British needs, pig iron and iron bar made in the colonies were permitted to enter England duty free. Parliament was somewhat divided, however. In the petition against allowing America's iron industry to grow it was argued that:

"The Encouraging of the Making of Iron in America, will put them upon Manufacturing, and they will supply them selves first, and all of the Colonies; so that the Manufacturers here must starve."

A petition offered in contrast argued that:

"To forbid his Majesty's Subjects the making of any sort of Iron Wares when its for their own Necessary Use and not for Exportation, seems to bear hard on the common Rights and Liberties of Mankind; especially, when the Ore is what their own Soil yields, and what is found but in small Quantities comparatively in the Mother Kingdom."

Smelting a ton of iron required about 140 bushels of charcoal drawn from five cords of wood (a cord is an amount of stacked wood measuring 8 feet by 4 feet by 4 feet). It was considered necessary to devote at least four square miles of woodland as the basic supply source for each furnace built. Burning wood into charcoal became an industry itself— one that not only rapidly deforested the wilderness but greatly polluted the air.

By the mid-1770s colonies maintained 82 charcoal-fueled furnaces, 175 forges, and a large number of bloomeries (simple furnaces used for smelting iron). The total output in the colonies was greater than that of England and Wales, and represented about one-seventh of the world's supply.

Labor for furnaces was furnished by slaves, some of whom became experts in the field. It took up to 120 slaves to run some of the larger furnaces.

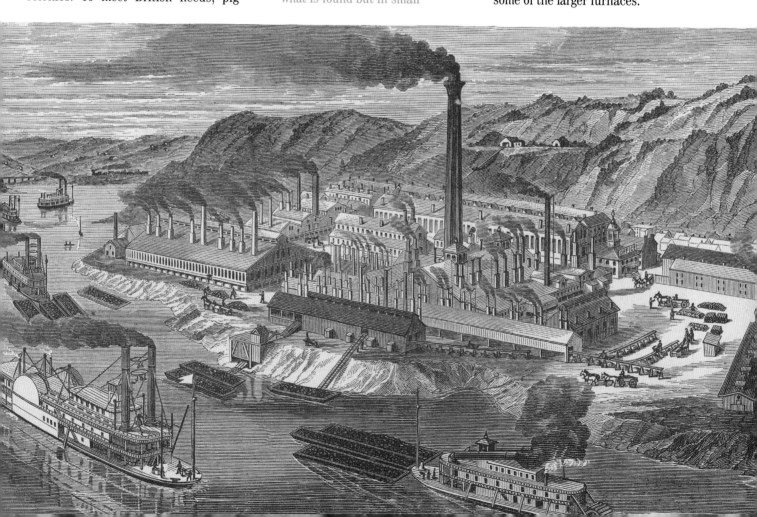

Governor Spotswood

Although the colorful Alexander Spotswood is perhaps best known as colonial governor of Virginia (1710–1722), he was—among other things—an important figure in establishing the iron industry in the American colonies, expanding the settlement of Virginia, and even curbing the pirate trade.

Spotswood also is considered the first representative of the British government in America to fully appreciate the value of the western territory. Spotswood encouraged settlement of the frontier by exempting settlers from taxes and quitrents (a form of rent paid by a free man instead of services required by feudal custom).

During his years as governor Spotswood took several opportunities to mix opportunities for personal gain with his official duties. In 1714 he established the Germanna Colony, peopled by 40 supposedly abandoned German immigrants on land he controlled. He described the colony and the efforts as "protecting the frontier," but it was in reality an effort to develop an early iron furnace (despite British opposition) and develop rich deposits on his land using cheap labor.

John Fontaine visited the Germanna settlement in November 1715, reporting that "the Germans live very miserably." The town, he wrote:

> "Is pallisaded with stakes stuck in the ground, and laid close the one to the other, of substance to bear out a musket shot. There is but nine families and they have nine houses built all in a line, and before every house about 20 feet from the house they have small sheds built for their hogs and hens, so that the hog stys and houses make a street. This place that is paled in is a pentagon, very regularly laid out, and in the very centre there is a blockhouse made with five sides which answers to the five sides of pales or great inclosure. There is loop holes through it, from which you may see all the inside of the inclosure. This was intended for a retreat for the people in case they were not able to defend the pallisades if attacked by the Indians. They make use of this Blockhouse for divine service."

In 1716 Spotswood led an expedition into the Shenandoah Valley. Apparently the real point of this "expedition" was a public relations trip for Spotswood. He wanted to open up the frontier of Virginia to settlers and to promote the usefulness of his iron furnace. There also was much merriment on this foray. Fontaine maintained a journal during the trip and made the notation:

> "I graved my name on a tree by the river side; and the Governor buried a bottle with a paper inclosed, on which he writ that he took possession of this place in the name and for King George the First of England. We had a good dinner, and after it we got the men together, and loaded all their arms, and we drank the King's health in champagne, and fired a volley—the Princess's health in Burgundy, and fired a volley, and all the rest of the Royal Family in claret, and a volley. We drank the Governor's health and fired another volley. We had several sorts of liquors, viz., Virginia red wine and white wine, Irish usquebaugh, brandy, shrub, two sorts of rum, champagne, canary, cherry, punch, water, cider."

Spotswood also kept an eye on the coast. Frustrated with piracy along the eastern seaboard that was damaging Virginia commerce, Governor Spotswood decided it was time for action—possibly motivated at least in part by publicity. His target was the high-profile pirate Blackbeard. Spotswood knew Blackbeard's sympathizers included Virginia leaders and businessmen. So in early November 1718 he secretly commissioned two ships to specifically hunt down and kill Blackbeard and his crew. Weeks after the ships sailed, Spotswood made a public proclamation:

"It is, amongst other things enacted, that all and every Person, or Persons who... shall take any Pyrate, or Pyrates, on the Sea or Land, or in Case of Resistance, shall kill any such Pyrate, or Pyrates...shall be entitled to have, and receive out of the publick Money, in the Hands of the Treasurer of this Colony, the several Rewards following; that is to say, for Edward Teach, commonly call'd Captain Teach, or BlackBeard, one hundred Pounds, for every other Commander of a Pyrate Ship, Sloop, or Vessel, forty Pounds; for every Lieutenant, Master, or Quarter-Master, Boatswain, or Carpenter, twenty Pounds; for every other inferior Officer, fifteen Pounds, and for every private Man taken on Board such Ship, Sloop, or Vessel, ten Pounds."

At the end of his governorship in 1722 Spotswood remained in Virginia near his ironworks, having acquired a vast amount of land in Spotsylvania County (named after him). In 1730 he was made deputy postmaster general of the American colonies and served in that role until 1739. It was Spotswood who promoted Benjamin Franklin to the position of postmaster for the province of Pennsylvania Franklin later became postmaster general of the colonies. Spotswood died in 1740.

BELOW: **A sailor fights Blackbeard, on the deck of a ship. Blackbeard was killed by sailors sent from Virginia in 1718.**

SLAVERY AND MANUFACTURING

"How is it that we hear the loudest yelps for liberty among the drivers of Negroes?"

Samuel Johnson, English writer and dictionary maker, asked this question on the eve of revolution in 1775. To some there was an obvious contrast between the noble aims of the American Revolution and the presence of slightly more than a half-million enslaved African Americans in the 13 colonies. Slavery was practiced in every colony at that time and was essential to most of the leading industries, including tobacco, cotton, indigo, rice, and naval stores. In other words, it was the key to most of the early riches of the colonies.

Slavery in America—often called the "peculiar institution"—developed in a manner most unusual to the world. Arguably the earliest of American slaves were the white indentured servants, who were essentially "owned" until earning their freedom over a period averaging 5

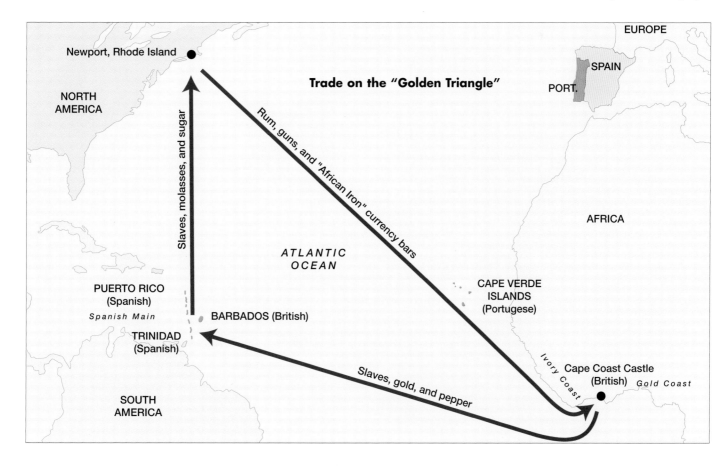

Trade on the "Golden Triangle"

EUROPE

SPAIN

PORT.

Newport, Rhode Island

NORTH AMERICA

Slaves, molasses, and sugar

Rum, guns, and "African Iron" currency bars

ATLANTIC OCEAN

AFRICA

PUERTO RICO (Spanish)

Spanish Main

BARBADOS (British)

CAPE VERDE ISLANDS (Portugese)

TRINIDAD (Spanish)

Slaves, gold, and pepper

Ivory Coast

Cape Coast Castle (British) *Gold Coast*

SOUTH AMERICA

BELOW LEFT: **The so-called "Golden Triangle." Slaves were brought from Africa and traded in the West Indies for molasses and sugar, which was then traded (along with slaves) to Americans for rum. The rum was taken back to Africa to trade for more slaves.**

LEFT: **An instrument of coercion.**

RIGHT: **A Dutch man-of-war unloading slaves in Virginia. It may well show the first shipment of slaves to America in 1619.**

to 7 years. Other early "slaves" included the so-called "tobacco wives" and imported orphans from England. These people also earned their "freedom," although the word may have meant little to wives of the time.

Much of America's early wealth was built on the labor of imported, indentured Europeans and, later, black Africans. Unlike the whites, early black slaves did not choose to emigrate—they were captured from their native African villages. But like the white indentured servants, they were, at first, able to earn their freedom over time. In all cases slave labor—black and white—earned masters rich rewards, creating a culture in which slavery became necessary.

The first black slaves

The first recorded black African slaves arrived in the colonies on August 20, 1619, in Jamestown, Virginia. John Rolfe's journal refers to "a Dutch man-of-warre that sold us 20 negars." These early slaves were treated as indentured servants that were eventually set free.

Slavery as we now visualize it didn't begin to develop until the latter part of the seventeenth century. Oddly enough, it did not develop through racist attitudes but by financial necessity and the lust for profit. Especially ironic is the fact that the first slave for life in the colonies—John Casor—was owned by a free black slave owner, Anthony Johnson, of Northampton, Virginia. In 1655

Johnson won a court battle and a declaration that stated "hee had ye Negro [Casor] for his life."

During the early years slaves were treated differently in different areas of the colonies. Many blacks in New York were free, and those who weren't did not seem to be treated any worse than indentured servants. The Pennsylvania Quakers, who held that "all men are created equal," seemed to have little problem accepting slavery.

However, the Chesapeake is the one area where there was—almost from the

beginning—slavery and prejudice. Most owners in the northern colonies seemed to treat slaves with as much fairness as they would indentured servants or family. The same seemed to be true of most of the southern colonies for the better part of a century.

In 1745 Eliza Lucas, who was responsible for the successful cultivation of the indigo plant, wrote:

"I am resolved to make a good Mistress to my servants, to treat them with humanity and good

nature; to give them sufficient and comfortable clothing and provisions, and all things necessary for them. To be careful and tender of them in their sickness, to reprove them for their faults, to encourage them when they do well, and pass over small faults; not to be tyrannical, peevish or impatient towards them, but to make their lives as comfortable as I can."

Long parts of her day were devoted "to our little Polly [her sister] and two black girls who I teach to read." Lucas later created a school for slaves in her area with the two girls she taught to read serving as teachers.

Unfortunately Lucas was in a small minority of eighteenth-century slave owners who were kind. By this time slaves were property. And while property must be maintained, maintenance is a cost, and costs must be controlled. For example, Samuel Wilson, writing of the proprietary colony of Clarendon (now South Carolina), noted:

"Negroes by reason of the mildness of the winter thrive and stand much better than any in the more northern colonies, and require less clothes, which is a great charge saved."

From its early beginnings slavery grew rapidly in the American colonies, mostly due to the highly labor-intensive crops such as tobacco, rice, cotton, and indigo. Regardless of treatment, being a slave meant hard, year-round, lifelong labor. In 1761 South Carolina Governor Glen remarked:

"Both Indigo and Rice may be managed by the same Persons, for the Labour attending Indigo being over in the Summer Months, those who were employed in it may afterwards manufacture Rice in the ensuing Part of the Year, when it becomes most laborious; and after doing all this, they will have some Time to spare for sawing Lumber and making Hogsheads, and other Staves to supply the Sugar Colonies."

Unquestionably, slaves on dual-crop plantations lived hard lives of unceasing labor.

By the time the American Revolu-

SELLING SLAVES

Two advertisements from a colonial-era broadside newspaper: one for a cargo of slaves on the ship *Two Brothers*, and one for "Thirty Seasoned Negroes," including a carpenter, a cook, and his family.

LEFT: An African-American slave is sold at an auction in South Carolina, while a family looks on in despair. One potential buyer is examining the man's legs for strength.

tion began, there were slightly more than a half million slaves in the colonies. Some of the northern states were already beginning to question slave ownership, and many blacks fought in the Revolutionary War.

Arming slaves

In 1779 in response to a request to arm slaves to fight the British, Alexander Hamilton wrote:

"I have not the least doubt that the Negroes will make very excellent soldiers, with proper management … I hear it frequently objected to the scheme of embodying Negroes, that they are too stupid to make soldiers. This is so far from appearing to me a valid objection …for their natural faculties are as good as ours."

Hamilton went on to state that if Patriots didn't use black soldiers the British would, and that such an effort would likely help obtain their freedom. Hamilton wrote:

"This will secure their fidelity, animate their courage, and, I believe, will have a good influence upon those that remain, by opening a door to their emancipation."

In 1783 Massachusetts became the first state to abolish slavery, and numbers soon began to decline in several states—although it would take the better part of another century to finally eliminate the "peculiar institution" from America.

THE ROAD FROM FREEDOM TO SLAVERY

Olaudah Equiano, kidnapped with his sister in 1756 from Benin (part of Nigeria), described his capture as follows:

"I saw one of those people come into the yard of our next neighbor….Immediately I gave the alarm and he was surrounded by the stoutest, who entangled him with cords so that he could not escape till some of the grown people came and secured him.

"One day, when all our people were gone out to their works as usual, and only I and my sister were left to mind the house, two men and a woman got over our walls, and in a moment seized us both; and without giving us time to cry out or to make any resistance, they stopped our mouths and ran off with us into the nearest wood. Here they tied our hands, and continued to carry us as far as they could till night came on.

"The first object which saluted my eyes when I arrived on the coast was the sea, and a slave ship, which was then riding at anchor and waiting for its cargo. These filled me with astonishment, which was soon converted into terror when I was carried on board. I was immediately handled, and tossed up to see if I was sound, by some of the crew; and I was now persuaded that I had got into a world of bad spirits, and that they were going to kill me.

"When I looked round the ship and saw a large furnace boiling and a multitude of black people of every description chained together…I no longer doubted my own fate; and, quite overpowered with horror and anguish, I fell motionless on the deck and fainted."

COERCION

These woodcuts, of about 1750, show an iron mask and collar used by slaveholders to keep field workers from running away. These devices also were designed to prevent slaves from eating crops such as sugar cane. The mask made breathing difficult and, if left on too long, would tear away at the slave's skin when removed.

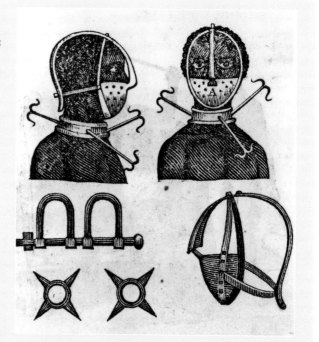

INDIGO

Indigo, a bushy plant that is cultivated and used to create blue dye, became a staple crop in eighteenth-century South Carolina. The plant, a perennial type of legume, was not native to America and owes its success specifically to Eliza Lucas.

Eliza's father, Colonel George Lucas, left her to tend to her frail mother, younger sister, three plantations, and 20 slaves when he went to Antigua to fight for the British against Spain in 1740. She was just 16. Eliza recalled:

> "I was very early fond of the vegetable world....When he [George] went to the West Indies, he sent me a variety of seeds, among them, indigo."

In July 1739 Eliza reported to her father that of indigo, ginger, cassava, and cotton she:

> "Had greater hopes from the Indigo—if I could have the seed earlier the next year from the West India's—than any of ye rest of ye things I had tryd."

At the time, Britain was forced to purchase all its indigo from France. Lucas wanted to change that, but it wasn't easy. The first year's crop froze, the second was ruined by worms, and the third saw only 100 plants survive to harvest. Eliza's father, trying to be

LEFT: **The indigo plant.**

BELOW LEFT: **The process of cloth dyeing has been practiced for many years. This shows the famous French cloth factory owned by the Gobelins family. Such factories relied heavily on the unique blue color produced by the indigo plant.**

BELOW RIGHT: **Wild Indigo in bloom.**

helpful, sent a dyemaster who deliberately ruined an entire year's harvest.

During the mid-1740s the war with the Spanish crippled South Carolina's economy. A Spanish naval blockade prevented rice crops from reaching the West Indies, leading to great hardship. South Carolina's dependency on rice was too great.

The first successful crop

In 1744 Lucas had her first successful indigo crop and distributed seeds free to her neighbors. In 1745, 5,000 pounds of indigo were exported, and by 1747 more than 130,000 pounds were exported. Within a few years Britain was no longer dependent on the French. In 1748 Governor James Glen advised the colonial assembly that "our success in indigo seems to be certain." Indigo, which grows on high, dry ground, complemented the rice plantations of the marshes. The two lucrative crops transformed South Carolina into one of the wealthiest of the 13 colonies. By the time of the Revolution, South Carolina was exporting 500,000 pounds of indigo per year, accounting for more than one-third of the colony's annual revenue.

As with rice and cotton, however, indigo was a labor-intensive crop. One slave could handle about two acres, which produced about 16 pounds of dye from three to five cuttings per year.

Dye extraction was done in large vats. John Stedman, writing in 1796, described the process as follows:

"The whole crop is tied in bunches, and put into a very large tub with water, covered over with very heavy logs of wood by way of pressers: thus kept, it begins to ferment; in less than 18 hours the water seems to boil, and becomes of a violet or garter blue colour.…The liquor is drawn off into another tub, which is something less, when the remaining trash is carefully picked up and thrown away; and the very noxious smell of this refuse it is that occasions the peculiar unhealthiness.…Being now in the second tub, the mash is agitated by paddles…all the grain separates from the water, the first sinking like mud to the bottom, while the latter appears clear and transparent on the surface: this water, being carefully removed till near the coloured mass, the remaining liquor is drawn off into a third tub, to let what indigo it may contain also settle in the bottom; after which…the sediment or indigo is put into proper vessels to dry, where being divested of its last remaining moisture, and formed into small, round, and oblong square pieces, it is become a beautiful dark blue, and fit for exportation."

Evaporation vats were usually located at least a quarter mile downwind of any home, due to the foul odor. It was generally thought that the fumes were fatal to many slaves. James Roberts, an African American who fought in the War of 1812, stated that:

"From fifty to sixty hands work in the indigo factory; and such is the effect of the indigo upon the lungs of the laborers, that they never live over seven years. Every one [slave] that runs away, and is caught, is put in the indigo fields, which are hedged all around, so that they cannot escape again."

Indigo was the basis of all fine blue colors, including that found on our own flag. The dye also played a role in the American Revolution. It was used to color blue coats that became the uniform of the Continental Army (in contrast to the British "red-coats").

Supporting the Patriots

Eliza Lucas was a British officer's daughter, but she supported the Patriot cause. She was already a widow by the time the Revolution began (her husband, Charles Pinckney, died in 1758), and she saw her plantations destroyed by British raiders. Her two sons also made notable contributions. Charles Cotesworth Pinckney fought in the Continental Army and signed the U.S. Constitution. Thomas Pinckney also fought in the Revolution and later became governor of South Carolina. When Eliza died of cancer in 1793, George Washington requested to serve as one of her pallbearers.

NAVAL STORES

"Naval stores" is the collective name for products such as tar, pitch, spirits of turpentine, and rosin—all of which are obtained from the pine tree. These products were needed for caulking wooden ships and waterproofing canvas sails of the seagoing vessels of the Royal British Navy in the seventeenth century.

Early explorers in the New World immediately saw the potential of the colonial forests for providing naval stores to Britain. Philip Amadas and Arthur Barlow, exploring the coastal forests of what is now North Carolina, reported in 1584 to Sir Walter Raleigh that they found:

> "Trees which could supply the English Navy with enough tar and pitch to make our Queen the ruler of the seas."

Captain John Smith was charged with extracting turpentine from the trees of Virginia and was provided with the following instructions:

> "Pyne trees, or ffir trees, are to be wounded within a yarde of the grounde, or boare a hoal with an agar the third pte into the tree, and lett yt runne inyo anye thinge that may receyve the same, and that such issues owte will be Turpentyne worthe 18 pounds per Tonne. When the tree beginneth to runne softelye it is to be stopped up agayne for preserveinge the tree."

The first recorded shipload of naval stores left Virginia bound for Britain in 1608.

Exports of tar

As colonies developed to the north, the attention of British shipbuilders naturally turned to the New England forests. Ultimately, New England forests couldn't provide the necessary supply; most of those resources went directly into New England shipbuilding efforts. Instead, it was the highly resinous wood (often called fatwood or lightwood) of the longleaf pine that sparked the naval stores industry. These trees were very common in the dense southern forests.

The industry prospered in the South until the forests began to become exhausted.

Between 1701 and 1718 American shipments of tar went from 177 to 82,000 barrels. In 1724 South Carolina alone exported 52,000 barrels, but this growth didn't continue. In 1768 the total tar exports to England from the colonies were slightly more than 135,000 barrels. Within two years that number had fallen down to about 102,000 barrels. England offered bounties—or incentive payments—to increase that number and stimulate the industry, which was quite profitable for those who continued to produce these products.

As relations grew tense between America and Britain, America began to cut off exports of naval stores that until that time, accounted for close to 80 percent of Britain's supply.

Distilling gum

To produce various forms of naval stores, gum from the longleaf pine was distilled into rosin and spirits of turpentine in what has been described by many as an "oversized liquor still." The process, described in the 1777 journal of traveler Ebenezer Hazard, was somewhat crude:

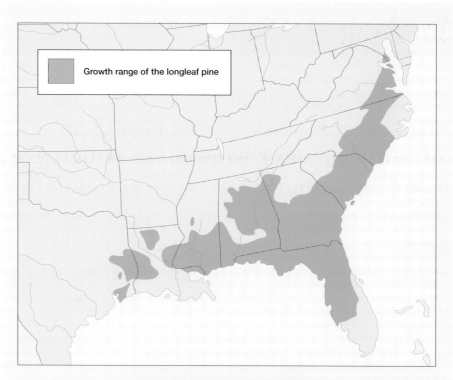

THE LONGLEAF PINE FOREST

Historians have estimated that the size of the early longleaf pine forest was between 70 and 90 million acres. Today, only slightly more than 3 million acres still exist (less than 4 percent). Furthermore, only about 1,000 acres of that number are virgin woods, that is, pristine and undisturbed. The rest are "second growth" (meaning they've been logged at least once). The American longleaf pine forest is considered among the most diverse of all forest systems. It supports hundreds of plant and animal species that are specially adapted to the conditions in healthy longleaf forests. Many of them are now threatened or endangered.

"I find that Tar & Turpentine are the Staple of the South Parts of Virginia…I saw great Numbers of Pines which were cut to get Turpentine: a large Notch is cut in the Trees cross-wise, the lower Part of which is hollowed to receive the Turpentine; a pretty large Slip is cut off the Tree on the upper Part of the Notch—Tar is made by taking a Parcel of Pine Knots or other Parts of the Trees which contain a large Quantity of Turpentine, & piling them up, covering & burning them in the same Manner as Blacksmiths in the Country usually do their Wood which they intend for Charcoal: A Trough is dug all round the Pile, with Drains communicating with both, which all empty themselves into a large Hole, from which the Tar is taken out & put into Barrels. The Coals serve for the same Purposes with other Charcoal."

The collection and processing of pine gum was a year-round ordeal and often required a large work force. Laborers would work their way from tree to tree chipping shallow gutters (called streaks) into the fresh wood of the tree face with a tool called a hack. This cut face and aluminum gutters nailed to the tree would direct the gum down into a "box" that was notched at the bottom of the tree by a broad axe. However, these boxes were often very destructive—essentially girdling the tree at its base. The cut faces were sometimes called "catfaces." North Carolina eventually got its nickname—the Tarheel State—because of the sticky resin that collected on barefoot workers' feet.

ABOVE LEFT AND LEFT: **"Middies" (midshipmen) learning the ropes at the naval school on board the USS Constitution.**

SHIPBUILDING

Perhaps because ships brought the original colonists to America from Britain, sea vessels were never far from colonists' minds. Although shipbuilding in the American colonies didn't become a true industry until the mid-1600s, ships were built from the earliest days—but there were a few false starts.

The first ship built in the colonies was the *Virginia*, built in 1607 in the colony that provided its name. Although it wasn't designed for deep oceangoing, the *Virginia* made two trips across the ocean to England. The Dutch on Manhattan Island launched their first ship, *Onrust*, in 1614.

In 1620 several British shipwrights came to the Jamestown colony to begin what they hoped would be a successful shipbuilding business but were able to complete only a couple of small vessels called shallops.

Meanwhile, the Plymouth Pilgrims hoped that a ship carpenter who arrived there in 1624 would get the industry going. He built several shallops and two ketches (small, two-masted ships) but died soon after. In 1626 they lengthened one of the shallops by sawing it and adding planks.

Finally, in 1629 it appeared as though the colonial shipbuilding effort could finally get underway when the Salem, Massachusetts, colonists lured six master ship carpenters to settle there by offering land and favors.

But the beginning of the true shipbuilding industry is credited to the

LEFT: **John Fitch—builder of the first steamship—is shown in the only portrait ever published. The portrait is taken from** *Lloyds Steamboat Directory.*

BELOW LEFT: **This early engraving of Charleston Harbor show ships of varying sizes, although all are quite small by today's standards.**

BELOW: **The USS** *Constitution* **is ready for launching after repairs in a navy yard. May 27, 1858.**

Puritans of Medford, Massachusetts. Their shipwrights managed to build a 30-ton merchant vessel that was launched in 1631. The ship was named *The Blessing of the Bay.*

Forests perfect for shipbuilding

Throughout the early colonies there were dense, mature forests of hardwoods that were perfect for shipbuilding. Forests of the North had tall white pines for masts and huge oak trees for hulls, including white oak with "knotless trunks fifty to seventy feet high."

The southern forests were largely mature woods composed of yellow and longleaf pines and various hardwoods, including white oak, chestnut, and walnut. Many of these monster trees were more than 90 feet tall, with trunks that were 16–20 feet in circumference. Many were close to 400 years old. It wasn't uncommon for branches to be at least 20 feet above ground, and it was often said that a squirrel could travel hundreds of miles without touching the ground. Clearly, the materials existed for a successful industry.

The longleaf pine in particular was important to shipbuilders. The wood itself is quite dense, rigid, and said to be as strong as red oak; and it is naturally resistant to rot, decay, and insects. The longleaf pine's tall, straight trunks multiplied the value of the lumber. Longleaf masts consistently sold in England for 25 to 30 percent more than those from other types of North American pine trees. In fact, the keel of the USS *Constitution* (known as Old Ironsides) was made from the timber of a single longleaf pine. Longleaf planks were used for its deck.

By 1641 shipbuilding (at least for smaller ships) was already a major New England industry. It was frequently noted that "one seems never to get away from the sound of the shipbuilder's hammer, and the rush of the launching vessel." That same year (1741) a Massachusetts law called for the inspection of all ships over 30 tons:

> "The building of ships is a business of great importance for the common good…therefore suitable care ought to be taken that it be well performed."

Larger ships

The year 1641 also signaled a change in the industry, as a 300-ton cargo vessel—the largest built in the colonies to that time—was launched. Within another three years New England shipbuilders had produced the 300-ton *Welcome*, 200-ton *Trial*, and 400-ton *Seaforth*. Shipyards continued to spring up around the colonies.

In 1690 the British Admiralty contracted with a Portsmouth, New Hampshire, shipyard to build a man-of-war. This was the first time a British naval vessel had been built outside the

British Isles. It was felt that since the ship was supposed to patrol New England waters, it could be built cheaper and more efficiently in the colonies, using colonial raw materials. Within a year the *Falkland* was launched. Other British naval vessels would soon be built in the colonies as well.

American shipbuilding became so successful that by the 1720s, British shipbuilders were complaining that the crown was favoring American colonial shipbuilders—a charge that was probably true, since the cheap raw materials allowed American shipbuilders to build quality vessels at less than two-thirds the cost of those built by the British.

The British government turned a deaf ear to the complaints, despite the fact that numerous shipwrights were heading to the colonies. Since Britain's primary and most profitable business was shipping, it needed a constant supply of good ships at the cheapest possible price. The industry continued to grow in the colonies, and by 1750 virtually every major port had a shipbuilding operation. After that the British began to cut back on their dependence on American-made ships because of a British belief that American wood was inferior. In reality it wasn't the wood that was inferior. Because demand was so great, lumber wasn't allowed to cure (dry) long enough, leading to warping, rot, and other problems that took ships out of commission for repair.

Nonetheless, by the time war broke out, at least one-third of Britain's merchant fleet was still being built in the colonies.

The Revolutionary War

Ironically, when the Revolutionary War began, the colonists found themselves facing the largest navy in the world—sporting a number of ships they built—yet America didn't yet have a regular navy. The Marine Committee of the Continental Congress did, however, take over and arm about 2,000 private merchant ships. These independently owned small warships were called privateers. Although such vessels couldn't face British warships, they could easily outmaneuver and destroy British merchant vessels attempting to deliver supplies to the British army. This was a significant contribution to the war.

During the war the Continental Congress ordered the construction of 13 frigates. Only eight could be built in time. Of those, two were captured—the *Hancock* and the *Providence*—and were so well built they were added to the British fleet.

The end of the Revolutionary War brought a boon to American shipbuilders. Since Americans were no longer limited in their trading—merchants were free

to trade any-where—a huge demand existed for new merchant vessels. Also, the rapidly growing whaling trade demanded ships. With minor interruptions the ship-building industry continued to be highly successful in America.

The steamship arrives

After mastering their shipbuilding skills with wind-driven vessels, Americans explored the idea of self-propelled boats. Plans for American steam-propelled vessels are known as early as 1736, but the first successful steamship, *The Experiment*, was built by John Fitch and launched on the Delaware River in August 1787. At the time, it traveled at about three miles per hour. By 1790 adjustments to the vessel allowed it to travel at eight miles per hour; it was time to go commercial. An advertisement in Philadelphia newspapers on July 14, 1790, stated:

"The Steamboat is now ready to take passengers and is intended to set off from Arch Street Ferry, in Philadelphia, every Monday, Wednesday, and Friday for Burlington, Bristol, Bordentown, and Trenton, to return on Tuesdays, Thursdays, and Saturdays."

Although this was the first commercial steamboat service, it operated at a loss, and, with several mishaps, Fitch's company went under.

A vessel of note appeared in the early 1790s, built by Samuel Morey. In 1797 his side-wheel steamer appeared on the Delaware River. According to Morey:

"The shaft ran across the boat with a crank in the middle, worked from the beam of the engine with a shackle bar."

Although it was an advanced design, nothing further came of it.

It was Robert Fulton, however, who built on his predecessor's experiments to create the first truly successful steamboat. The *Clermont* appeared August 17, 1807, near Greenwich Village, New York, headed for Albany. One viewer described the vessel as "looking precisely like a backwards saw-mill mounted on a scow and set on fire." In 1811, Fulton designed the *New Orleans*, which was the first steamboat to operate on the Mississippi River—and we were off!

BELOW LEFT: **This dramatic painting by Michele Felice Corne (about 1814) shows the USS *Constitution* in action with HMS *Guerriere*, August 19, 1812.**

BELOW: **This undated painting shows Robert Fulton's *Clermont* on the river. Note the misspelling of the ship's name on the bow.**

The American Industrial Revolution began shortly after the close of the American Revolution. It started in the textile industry, where a series of inventions created new demands for laborers.

The young nation began as a weak, loose association of former colonies with a traditional economy. More than three-quarters of the labor force still worked in agriculture in 1790.

By the 1780s the British knew how to harness water power to operate equipment that spun cotton into yarn. America was still using hand spinning wheels. Obviously such a technological advantage also was a huge economical advantage for Britain, and it wished to protect it. Thus Britain not only forbade workers to leave the country but also prohibited exporting machine parts. Soon American manufacturers were offering huge rewards for anyone who could design an English-style mill. Samuel Slater, a young man not yet 21, was apprenticed in a British spinning mill and was extremely familiar with their workings. He memorized them and moved to America in disguise, helping to build British-style mills in the Providence, Rhode Island, area.

Child labor

In December 1790 four boys made history in Pawtucket, Rhode Island, when they became America's first factory workers at a spinning mill operated by Slater. One of the boys, 10-year-old Smith Wilkinson, was told by Slater how to operate his area. His instructions would likely have been as follows:

> "First, take up a handful of cotton and pull it apart with both hands. Put it all into your right hand, then feed the cotton into your machine by moving your hand back and forth over the frame that sorts cotton. That's it. Just keep doing it."

Wilkinson did, in uncomfortable conditions for more than 14 hours a day six days a week. Within a few more days five more children between the ages of 7 and 12 joined the ranks, forming America's first mechanical factory work force.

Within 10 years there were 100 children working at the factory. The youngest was only four. James Horton, a boy who later quit Slater's mill, said:

> "If Mr. Slater had taught me to work all the different branches I [would still be] with you now. But instead, he kept me always at one thing and I might have stood there until this time and never knew nothing."

As the industry grew and other types of factories appeared, mill owners began hiring more and more women and children as workers. They not only felt they were helping children build character through hard work, but women and children worked more cheaply than men. Families began to live off the fruits of their exhausted children.

In 1793 the cotton gin, an ingeniously simple machine invented by young Yale graduate Eli Whitney, further simplified the system. One gin (engine) allowed a man to clean seeds from cotton 50 times faster than by hand. Once connected to a steam engine, the gin improved its speed by 20 times, allowing for one day's work to equal that of 1,000 men by hand.

Because of America's exploding textile industry created by Slater's mill and the cotton gin, a huge demand was created for more cotton, which had to be picked, cleaned, baled, loaded, and

LEFT: **Illustration of a cabinetmaker from Edward Hazen's *Book of Trades*, 1807. Furniture making was among the earliest forms of American manufacturing.**

BELOW: **An illustration of the power loom and Dr. Edmund Cartwright (1743–1823), English clergyman and the device's inventor.**

delivered. The slave trade, which had slowly begun to die out after the end of the Revolutionary War, came roaring back with a vengeance.

America's industrial revolution had truly arrived. Southern planters began buying up tillable property and planting cotton. By 1830 more than one million children worked in textile mills under less-than-humane conditions in many cases. The dresses, shirts, and other articles of clothing Americans were able to purchase had been created from cotton picked by slaves and worked into fabric and assembled by children.

SAMUEL SLATER (1768-1835)

Samuel Slater, founder of America's first true factory, also is recognized as founder of the cotton industry in the United States. As a young man who was not yet 21, Slater successfully smuggled the Industrial Revolution across the ocean. He was born in Belper, England, and was apprenticed at the age of 14 to the British inventor of cotton-spinning machinery, Sir Richard Arkwright. Slater became highly knowledgeable in improved textile machinery and was familiar with the inner workings of the British machines. Great Britain forbade its textile workers from leaving the country. The young United States offered handsome bounties for textile information for its growing industry, and Slater immigrated in disguise to America. He had memorized a lot of info-rmation on textile techniques and machine specifications. In 1790 Slater opened the first important spinning mill in the United States in Pawtucket, Rhode Island. The Sunday school he established in 1796 for his workers was one of the first such programs in America.

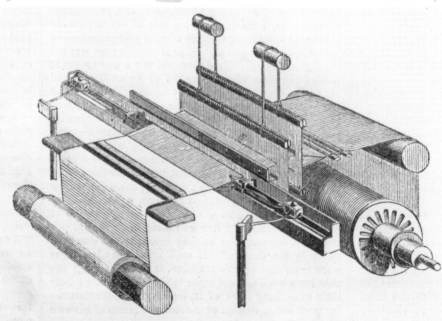

The Boston Manufacturing Company

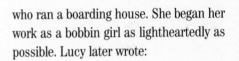

As a result of the birth of America's Industrial Revolution, spawned by Slater's mill in Pawtucket, Rhode Island, as well as the development of the cotton gin, textile mills almost seemed to spring from the ground throughout New England as America entered the nineteenth century.

One such mill was the Boston Manufacturing Company, founded in Waltham, Massachusetts. This mill, which revolutionized the textile industry, traced its beginnings to the War of 1812. The Boston Manufacturing Company was the beginning of integrated manufacturing; that is, all manufacturing steps were completed under one roof. Raw cotton entered the mill and came out as finished cloth. This important step in the American Industrial Revolution was made by 12 Boston merchants (headed by Francis Cabot Lowell) who sought to divert their money from shipping to manufacturing. They were looking for a different way to make money after a wartime British naval blockade threatened to choke their overseas trade. Construction on the mill, designed to manufacture cotton "sheeting" (a multipurpose cloth used primarily for slave clothing), began in 1813. Production of cloth started in 1814.

Nathan Appleton, one of the original businessmen who founded the mill commented on one of the looms, remarking about:

"The state of admiration and satisfaction with which we sat by the hour, watching the beautiful movement of this new and wonderful machine, destined as it evidently was, to change the character of all textile industry."

Appleton, of course, was not operating the loom. "There were 160 looms all going in that room," said one mill guide years later. "Stop and think about how loud it would have been when they didn't have earplugs."

The "Lowell Girls"

That incessant and extremely loud noise filled our nation's first planned industrial city and drew young women who became known as "Lowell Girls" to the mills. Eleven-year-old Lucy Larcom observed after her first day of work at the Boston Manufacturing Company:

"Why it is nothing but fun. It is just like play."

Both Lucy and her older sister, Linda, had applied to work, but only Lucy was hired because she was taller and looked older to the mill agent. But Lucy's opinion wasn't shared by all of the Lowell Girls, nor did her attitude stay so cheerful over time.

Lucy became a Lowell Girl to help ease the burden of support for her mother, who ran a boarding house. She began her work as a bobbin girl as lightheartedly as possible. Lucy later wrote:

"I went to my first day's work with a light heart. And it really was not so hard just to change bobbins on the spinning frames every three-quarters of an hour or so, with a half a dozen other girls who were doing the same thing."

But her work days began at 5 a.m. and frequently lasted until 7 p.m. or later:

"I defied the machinery to make me its slave. Its incessant discourds could not drown the music of my thoughts if I would let them fly high enough. The buzzing and hissing whizzing of pulleys and rollers and spindles and flyers often grew tiresome. I could not see into their complications or feel interested in them. When you do the same thing twenty times—a hundred times a day—it is so dull!"

Like other Lowell Girls, Lucy received a 15-minute breakfast break and a 30-minute break for lunch. Because early factories such as the Boston Manu-

facturing Company controlled virtually every aspect of an employee's life—from housing on—it was very difficult for the Lowell Girls to even begin to think of demanding better working conditions. The first strike didn't occur at the Boston Manufacturing Company until 1836.

ABOVE: **An 1835 engraving showing female workers at a textile factory in the process of preparing cotton.**

ABOVE LEFT: **An apprentice at his loom.**

RIGHT AND FAR RIGHT: **Though slightly outside our period, the** Lowell Offering **of December 1845 was "a repository of original articles written by the factory girls" that offered stories about a life of hard work that probably hadn't changed much since the mill opened in 1814.**

MANUFACTURING AND POLITICS

Manufacturing and politics have, since the dawn of American settlement, been very much entwined. Much of this is due to the fact that the British founded the American colonies under a system of mercantilism.

Mercantilism is a form of economic system in which the colonies' primary job is to supply natural resources to the factories of the home country (Britain). The home country would then fashion these raw materials into finished products that would be sold back to the colonies. In exchange the colonies received protection and guaranteed trade.

Almost from the beginning this system was at odds with the colonial spirit. It made little sense to entrepreneurial colonists to ship materials to England and wait many months for them to return as more expensive finished products. They were quite capable of fulfilling their own needs in fairly short order.

As British merchants and manufacturers became more concerned at the level of independent activity (and profits) in the colonies, the British government enacted more legislation to force the colonies to stick to its system.

Among the first of a number of acts that would severely raise the political hackles of the colonists was the Molasses Act of 1733. This was a tax slapped on foreign sugar sold in the British Empire. It forced Americans to buy expensive British West Indian sugar for their rum making. This not only made rum more expensive, it also cut colonial profits on its sale. Extensive smuggling resulted, and Molasses Act receipts fell dramatically.

As the crown became more nervous, other prohibitive acts came, including the Iron, Sugar, Stamp, Quartering, and Tea acts, among others. Each of them drove a fresh wedge between the manufacturing and political factions of the colonies and Britain. These acts hindered the development of manufacturing in the colonies and were a primary focus of the agitation preceding the American Revolution. Around the time of the Revolutionary War William Knox, a British official with much experience with the American colonies, noted of the colonists:

ABOVE: **Alexander Hamilton, by John Trumbull in 1806.**

BELOW: **View of the East Front of the President's House designed by Benjamin Henry Latrobe in 1807.**

"The seeds of disunion were sowed in the first plantation in every one of them, and that the general disposition to independence of this country prevailed throughout the whole."

His words couldn't have been more accurate. It was virtually impossible for the crown to expect colonists thousands of miles away to continue to be completely dependent on the mother country when they had the resources, talents, and most of all the need to manufacture products for their own consumption.

As tension built between Britain and America, colonists became more determined than ever to be independent—even if it meant with less finesse. Anna Green Winslow, 12-year-old daughter of a British military officer, in 1771 began to side with the colonists by joining a sewing circle. Sewing circles had been in existence since the late 1760s to protest British taxes. The women who belonged to these mild resistance groups made their own fabrics, clothes, and other household goods. Winslow wrote:

"As I am (as we say) a daughter of liberty I chuse to wear as much of our own manufactory as possible."

Thomas Jefferson's views on industry
Even after the Revolution Americans were still somewhat at odds with what was rapidly becoming a manufacturing economy. Thomas Jefferson strongly supported an agricultural focus and feared industry. One comment he made in 1816 showed this:

"To the labor of the husbandman, a vast addition is made by the spontaneous energies of the earth on which it is employed: for one grain of wheat committed to the earth, she renders twenty, thirty, and even fifty fold, whereas to the labor of the manufacturer nothing is added."

Of course, Jefferson was apparently not considering the labor of his slaves in this equation. Years earlier, in a 1787 letter to James Madison, Jefferson wrote:

"While we have land to labour then, let us never wish to see our citizens occupied at a work-bench, or twirling a distaff. Carpenters, masons, smiths, are wanting in husbandry: but, for the general operations of manufacture, let our work-shops remain in Europe. It is better to carry provisions and materials to workmen there, than bring them to the provisions and materials, and with them their manners and principles."

He felt the manufacturing life carried with it an immoral lifestyle.

The Federalists' view
On the other hand, George Washington, Alexander Hamilton, and other Federalists saw the need for a strong manufacturing base nurtured and supported by a strong central government. In a January 29, 1789, letter to Marquis de Lafayette, Washington wrote:

"Though I would not force the introduction of manufactures, by extravagant encouragements, and to the prejudice of agriculture; yet, I conceive much might be done in that way by women, children and others; without taking one really necessary hand from tilling the earth. Certain it is, great savings are already made in many articles of apparel, furniture and consumption. Equally certain it is, that no diminution in agriculture has taken place, at the time when greater and more substantial improvements in manufactures were making, than were ever before known in America."

Clearly Washington felt the two could co-exist—even if it meant using women and children in industry. He closed with a pro-American sentiment that still survives:

"I use no porter [beer] or cheese in my family, but such as is made in America: both those articles may now be purchased of an excellent quality."

BELOW: **An angry mob protests against the Stamp Act by throwing stamped documents onto a bonfire in Boston. The Stamp Act, a tax on documents and publications, was passed in 1765 by the British government to increase revenue from the colonies. It was repealed in 1799 after pressure from both sides of the Atlantic.**

Benjamin Franklin

Benjamin Franklin ranks among the best known of all colonial leaders. He was a statesman, inventor, and an extraordinary man.

Franklin's inventions include bifocals, the lightning rod, the Franklin stove, and the odometer. His innovations include daylight savings time, fire departments, political cartoons, and the effective use of vitamin C as a nutrient. Franklin's accomplishments during the Revolutionary War are also well known, but few know about his early life.

Franklin's numerous accomplishments in many different areas were not typical colonial behavior. To emphasize this, more than a century after Franklin's death Mark Twain wrote, with tongue in cheek:

"His simplest acts, also, were contrived with a view to their being held up for the emulation of boys forever—boys who might otherwise have been happy....He [Franklin] would work all day and then sit up nights and let on to be studying algebra by the light of a smouldering fire, so that all other boys might have to do that also."

Franklin, the third youngest of 17 children, became a printer—a trade very different from his father, who was a tallow chandler (dealer) and soap boiler. Printing came fairly naturally to the gifted boy. Franklin explains in his *Autobiography*:

"From a child I was fond of reading....This bookish inclination at length determined my father to make me a printer, tho' he already had one son (James) of that profession."

Franklin was indentured to his brother at age 12. Although James, who published the second newspaper of the colonies, *The New England Courant*, was frequently abusive to young Franklin, he did teach him much, including satire, criticism, and an "aversion to arbitrary power." Franklin soon began to write articles, sliding them anonymously under the door (fearing his brother wouldn't otherwise publish his work).

An unusual set of circumstances changed Franklin's course:

"One of the pieces in our newspaper, on some political point

ABOVE: **James Earl Fraser's statue of Benjamin Franklin in the Benjamin Franklin National Monument, Pennsylvania.**

LEFT: *Poor Richard's Almanack* **for the year 1773 (printed in 1772) by Benjamin Franklin (1706–1790). With its pithy sayings and memorable tales the *Almanack* espoused industry and frugality as the guide to a good life.**

Poor Richard, 1733.

AN

Almanack

For the Year of Chrift

1733,

Being the Firſt after LEAP YEAR:

And makes ſince the Creation **Years**
By the Account of the Eaſtern *Greeks*   7241
By the Latin Church, when ☉ ent. ♈ -   6932
By the Computation of *W. W.*   5742
By the *Roman* Chronology   5682
By the *Jewiſh* Rabbies   5494

Wherein is contained

The Lunations, Eclipſes, Judgment of the Weather, Spring Tides, Planets Motions & mutual Aſpects, Sun and Moon's Riſing and Setting, Length of Days, Time of High Water, Fairs, Courts, and obſervable Days.

Fitted to the Latitude of Forty Degrees, and a Meridian of Five Hours Weſt from *London*, but may without ſenſible Error, ſerve all the adjacent Places, even from *Newfoundland* to *South-Carolina*.

By *RICHARD SAUNDERS*, Philom.

PHILADELPHIA:
Printed and ſold by *B. FRANKLIN*, at the New Printing-Office near the Market.

The 18 months that Ben Franklin spent in London enabled him to rise to meet the challenges his emerging country in several ways—literally making him a founder of our nation. The term "founder" simply means to establish the basis of, as in foundation. But it also refers to one who casts in metal.

In the colonial printing trade printers used metal type to create printing plates. Until Franklin devised a way to cast, or found, lead type, after observing the process in England, all type was imported. With his innovation Franklin became the first letter founder in America. This led to less of a dependence on England. His keen sense of observation while in England also led to his contributions as a founding father during the American Revolution.

which I have now forgotten, gave offense to the Assembly. He [James] was taken up, censured, and imprisoned for a month by the Speaker's Warrant….I too was taken up and examined before the Council; but…they contented themselves with admonishing me, and dismissed me; considering me perhaps as an apprentice, who was bound to keep his master's secrets."

Franklin ran the paper in James's absence, taking a few editorial jabs at authority that Franklin felt made critics view him as "a young genius that had a turn for libelling and satire."

When the elder Franklin was released, it was under the condition that "James Franklin should no longer print the paper called the New England Courant." After some discussion it was decided the paper would continue, but published by "Benjamin Franklin." To avoid accusations that James was

publishing through his apprentice, Franklin's indenture was returned. Another private contract was drawn up between the brothers. "A very flimsy scheme it was," Franklin wrote.

Soon a dispute arose between the brothers. Franklin left the paper despite his private indenture, and an angry James kept Benjamin from being hired by other printers in Boston. A friend helped him go to New York (where he found no work) and then to Philadelphia. He was only 17.

In 1724, at age 18, Franklin went to England and spent 18 months working in London. Upon his return to Philadelphia Franklin again worked as a printer and began engraving and also casting type. Franklin wrote:

"I had seen types cast at St. James's in London, but without much attention to the matter. However, I now contrived a mold, made use of the letters we had, as puncheons, struck the matrices in lead, and thus supplied in a pretty

tolerable way all deficiencies. I also engraved several things on occasion. I made the ink, I was the warehouseman, and everything, in short quite a factotum."

He soon started his own paper, which grew quickly, "one of the good effects of having learned a little to scribble." Franklin felt another reason for his early success was that "the leading men, seeing a newspaper now in the hands of one who could also handle a pen, thought it convenient to oblige and encourage me."

"In 1732 I first printed my almanac, under the name of Richard Saunders; it was continued by me about 25 years, commonly called Poor Richard's almanac. I endeavored to make it both entertaining and useful, and it accordingly came to be in such demand that I reaped considerable profit from it, vending annually near ten thousand."

Arguably the printing trade was the most important of all colonial industries—not because it was the largest or the most profitable (it wasn't), but because of the power it wielded in gaining our independence from Britain.

Initially there were no presses in the colonies, and the industry was slow to materialize. Any need for printed goods—generally government documents or religious tracts—was handled by Britain (with the inevitable delays in waiting for two transatlantic passages). Newspapers didn't exist in the colonies. News was passed person to person or by the town crier.

However, educated men who saw the need for printing presses were present in the colonies from an early date. One of these individuals, Jesse (Jose) Glover, was a minister who traveled to England to obtain a printing press and an operator.

In 1638 Glover's widow (he died on the return voyage) returned to Cambridge, Massachusetts, with 18-year-old Stephen Daye (a locksmith by trade) and set up the first American press near the newly established Harvard College. The first document printed in the colonies was the *The Freeman's Oath*. These events were important enough to be noted in the 1639 journal of Massachusetts Governor John Winthrop:

"A printing house was begun at Cambridge by one Daye, at the charge of Mr. Glover, who died on sea hitherward. The first thing which was printed was the freeman's oath; the next was an almanack made for New England... the next was the Psalms newly turned into metre."

ENGRAVING AND OTHER PRINTING TECHNIQUES

Of the major printing types that are now used, only letterpress (raised-surface printing) and line-engraved intaglio (recessed printing) were in use during the American colonial years (lithography, or surface printing, wasn't invented until 1798). Letterpress printing, utilizing a raised printing surface, includes standard printing forms, cast letters, and woodcuts. The raised surface is inked and subsequently prints on the paper. Line engraving was generally reserved for security and art-related printing. Lines were incised into a steel die (in reverse). The die or (later) printing plate was then inked, wiped carefully to remove all excess ink, and then printed under pressure. Moistened paper pulls the ink from the engraved lines. Colonial newspapers, books, broadsides, and most currency were all printed by letterpress.

After completing *The Freeman's Oath* and the *Bay Book of Psalms*, the press kept busy producing numerous legal, religious, and scholarly works.

Soon a few other presses were established, but each was dependent on everyday works such as government papers, forms, almanacs, alphabet primers, sermons, and other bits of commercial paper for survival.

There was another problem with early colonial printing. There was no such thing as freedom of the press. Governors and others feared criticism—and thus printers—and consistently

attempted to censor their production. In 1671 Virginia Governor William Berkeley wrote:

> "I thank God, there are no free schools nor printing and I hope shall not have, these hundred years, for learning has brought disobedience, and heresy, and sects into the world, and printing has divulged them, and libels against the best government. God keep us from both."

Nonetheless, printers began to look toward the establishment of newspapers to inform and help shape public opinion. Between 1690 and 1820, more than 2,000 different newspapers appeared in America, indicating the great desire of people to have access to news. However, only about 400 of these newspapers lasted longer than 10 years.

By 1763 there were print shops in all 13 colonies, the last having been established in Savannah, Georgia, in 1762. At that time there were about 40 active presses in the colonies.

Press freedom

As the colonies drifted toward war with Britain, the press pushed for one very important principle—freedom. Despite the fact that most printers supported the Patriot effort, they realized that a nearly equal number of Tories, or British supporters, read their papers as well. To serve both audiences fairly, these printers remained as objective as possible in reporting about news, taxes, and other developing situations. This allowed their readers to form their own opinions.

Even a number of years before war broke out, there were significant struggles to avoid censorship. John Peter Zenger, a New York printer, was jailed and tried for libel by the colonial governor, William Cosby. In 1733 Zenger's paper, the *Weekly Journal*, reported on blatant attempts by Cosby to fix an election result. The paper also offered this eloquent statement on the importance of a free press:

> "The loss of liberty in general would soon follow the suppression of the liberty of the press; for it is an essential branch of liberty, so perhaps it is the best preservative of the whole. Even a restraint of the press would have a fatal influence. No nation ancient or modern has ever lost the liberty of freely speaking, writing or publishing their sentiments, but forthwith lost their liberty in general and became slaves."

A jury found Zenger innocent in his 1735 trial. As a result, the definition of libel (printed untruths) was changed, and

BELOW: **Printers operate presses in an eighteenth-century printing plant. The man second from left is inking the forms with leather daubers. The worker at right is operating the screw-action press.**

other printers realized that freedom of speech was no longer limited to the elite.

Common Sense

A few years later, in the heat of revolution, America had its first best-seller, Thomas Paine's *Common Sense*, which was published January 17, 1776. This pamphlet, dealing with British tyranny and the need for an independent republic, spoke in the language of the common man and grabbed the attention of many would-be Americans. Even today, the words are inspiring:

> "THESE are the times that try men's souls. The summer soldier and the sunshine patriot will, in this crisis, shrink from the service of their country; but he that stands it now, deserves the love and thanks of man and woman. Tyranny, like hell, is not easily conquered; yet we have this consolation with us, that the harder the conflict, the more glorious the triumph. What we obtain too cheap, we esteem too lightly: it is dearness only that gives every thing its value."

The pamphlet quickly sold more than 150,000 copies at a time when the circulation of most newspapers didn't exceed 2,000. Demand for Paine's passionate work soon exceeded the capacities of colonial printers, and it was read aloud in the streets. Within a year the pamphlet had gone through 25 printings, and many parts of it had been reproduced in colonial papers from Maine to Georgia.

Years later British historian George Trevelyan wrote that "it would be difficult to name any human composition which has had an effect so extended and so lasting."

The Massachusetts Spy

During the Revolution printer Isaiah Thomas's newspaper, the *Massachusetts*

THE COLONIAL GAZETTE

Num. 39.]   SUPPLEMENT.   Price 2 Pence

Oct.   1781

LETTER FROM GEN. WASHINGTON TO THE GOVERNOR OF MARYLAND, ANNOUNCING THE SURRENDER OF CORNWALLIS.

CAMP NEAR YORK, OCT., 1781.

DEAR SIR: Inclosed I have the honor of transmitting to your Excellency the terms upon which Lord Cornwallis has surrendered the Garrisons of York and Gloucester.

We have not been able yet to get an account of prisoners, ordnance or stores in the different departments; but from the best general report there will be (officers included) upwards of seven thousand men, besides seamen, more than 70 pieces of brass ordnance and a hundred of iron, their stores and other valuable articles.

My present engagements will not allow me to add more than my congratulations on this happy event, and to express the high sense I have of the powerful aid which i have derived from the State of Maryland in complying with my every request to the execution of it. The prisoners will be divided between Winchester, in Virginia, and Fort Frederick, in Maryland. With every sentiment of the most perfect esteem and regard, I have the honor to be

Your Excellency's most obedient and humble servant,   G. WASHINGTON.

The French at Yorktown.

Few things, indeed, suggested by the history of the war are more instructive than a parallel between the fate of Burgoyne and the fate of Cornwallis. The defeat of Washington on Long Island and the loss of New York had been attributed to the fact that his troops were raw militia. Yet it was mainly with just such men, and not with Continentals (as the regular soldiers of the united colonies were called), that the American commanders in northern New York overcame, in two successive battles, the well-disciplined and admirably appointed army of Burgoyne. This was the one brilliant military triumph achieved by either party in the whole course of the struggle; yet, strange to say, its most substantial fruit was its favorable effect on the negotiations which for two years Franklin had been pushing at the court of Versailles. It was not, however, until the beginning of the ensuing year that the French Ministry would even promise assistance to the colonies; and although their advances of money may from that time forward be said to have kept the continental army on its feet, they did not render effective military aid until the arrival of Count De Grasse in the Chesapeake, about the beginning of September, 1781.

The surrender of Cornwallis was the direct result of the advantage gained by De Grasse over Admiral Graves in the naval battle which took place off the mouth of Chesapeake Bay on September 5, 1781. For the first time during the war, the English failed to have a preponderance of naval strength in American waters, and for almost the first time an English Admiral, commanding a force not greatly inferior to his opponents, sailed pusillanimously away after an indecisive action, in which the French loss in killed and wounded was actually the greater. After this unexpected and inexcusable behaviour on the part of an English naval officer, the surrender of Cornwallis was clearly an obvious necessity. On one side there was the French fleet, comprising twenty four ships of the line

carrying 1,700 guns, and 19,000 seamen. On the land side was Rochambeau with French troops, aggregating 8,400 men, and 5,500 Continental troops under Washington, together with 3,000 militia, who were of less account. Against this military and naval force, Cornwallis had 7,500 men within the works of Yorktown, exclusive of 800 marines, disembarked from some English frigate which had lain in the river. Under these circumstances the surrender of the English force was plainly a mere question of time. It may be said, however, that the presence of the land force at a place where it could so happily co operate with the French fleet, bears witness to great strategical ability, and it has been usual to give the credit of the combination to Washington. It is clear, however, that throughout the summer of 1781, the American commander had not seriously contemplated anything but a concerted attack on Sir Henry Clinton in New York. From the day, however, that De Grasse arrived in the Chesapeake, and notified the American and French commanders that he would take his ships no further northward, it required no great strategist to perceive that the land forces must operate in Virginia, if at all. In that moment the objective point of Washington and Rochambeau was palpably the force which Cornwallis, in obedience to Clinton's orders, had collected at Yorktown. Cornwallis, on his part, because he counted notified in remaining on the peninsula, before, nor afterward, English fleet, and neither then, nor possible that an Admiral any Englishman have supposed it controlled would have acted possessing the armament which Graves Frenchmen till half of his ships were sunk.

In view of these facts, it behooves us in this great celebration at Yorktown, to render our French visitors the honors they deserve, for the event commemorated is more truly and emphatically a French than an American achievement.

Spy, was a highly popular paper that had him marked as a troublemaker. He once wrote that without a free press colonists would have:

> "Padlocks on our lips, fetters on our legs, and only our hands left at liberty to slave for our worse than Egyptian task masters."

In 1772 the *Massachusetts Spy* published a call to action "To the American Colonies" by a writer working under the pen name "Mucius Scaevola":

> "Your exertions in the great cause of freedom, have been noble; and they must be continued with redoubled vigor. The time is now come which requires your united strength and

THE PRESS

Early colonial printing presses differed very little from the fairly crude press used by Johannes Gutenburg to print the Bible back in the 1500s. The working parts of a press were iron, but all other construction was of wood. The lead type (letters) was imported from England until Benjamin Franklin was able to figure out how to cast type in the United States. Each letter was cast in hand-cut brass molds. A printer set up his plate by arranging the lead letters upside down and backward in a small brass pan called a stick. He then could check his accuracy by lightly inking the letters and "pulling" a crude "proof." Next a printer would wedge the arrangements of letters and words into an iron frame called a form, using spacers to help. The type form was placed on the bed of the press and inked with a filled leather dauber. Paper was then laid on the inked plate, and the iron platen was lowered by screw-action to pick up the impression from the form. Because the Continental Congress was unable to levy taxes to pay for the war, it relied on the printing press to issue nearly $250 million in paper money (the so-called Continental dollar). This early paper money was backed only by the good faith of the Continental Congress. There was too much money competing for too few goods, and the result was uncontrolled inflation. In early 1780 the Continental Congress confessed that its money was essentially worthless—something the colonists had known for a long time, as evidenced by their popular saying "not worth a Continental."

wisdom. Act agreeable to the character of Freemen, and you shall continue Free. You need not be instructed in the rights of mankind; you know them....If a clan of unrighteous men in Britain, with a few of their tools in America, should enslave this great, free, and growing people, astonishment must seize every generous mind, and all will view it as the most unaccountable event in the history of mankind. But it cannot be. Liberty has taken deep root, and will reign in America."

In the dead of night in 1775 Thomas shipped his press to Worcester, Massachusetts, where he produced the first printed account of the bloody beginning of the Revolutionary War at Lexington and Concord. The large headline read: "Americans!—Liberty or Death!—Join or Die!" After the war Thomas not only went on to establish the most successful printing operation in the young country, but he also produced the first illustrated Bible in America. It was hailed by Benjamin Franklin as "the most beautiful book produced in America."

ABOVE LEFT: **The power of the Press—the October 1781 *Colonial Gazette Supplement 39* features a letter from George Washington to the governor of Maryland announcing the surrender of Cornwallis.**

RIGHT: **A busy worker delivers paper in a wheelbarrow to the *Pennsylvania Gazette*.**

MANUFACTURING AND WAR

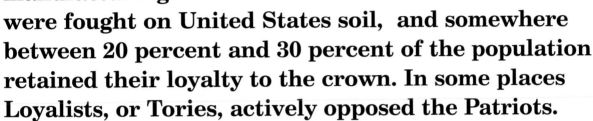

In many respects the Revolutionary War was a civil war, and civil wars typically have a huge effect on manufacturing. Most of the land battles were fought on United States soil, and somewhere between 20 percent and 30 percent of the population retained their loyalty to the crown. In some places Loyalists, or Tories, actively opposed the Patriots.

British General Charles Cornwallis directed Colonel Banastre Tarleton and his cavalry to destroy Virginia's few manufacturing centers and disrupt its government. Tarleton—known as "Bloody Ban"—was particularly hated for both his brutal tactics and the fact that his force was made up largely of American Loyalists. Tarleton's Dragoons advanced 70 miles in 24 hours, burning warehouses and seizing several plantations along the way.

John Hewson of Philadelphia became somewhat of a local hero during the Revolution. He opened a calico (cotton fabric with a bright pattern) printing factory in 1774 (the first in the colonies) near the Delaware River. An excerpt from his diary tells the story of his narrow escape from the British:

"When the British Army approached near to the city I removed with my family to the Jerseys about 4 miles from Cooper's Ferry; with my household furniture and as many of my manufacturing utensils as the shortness of the time would permit me to take, such as Copper boilers, and a large leaden vessel used in souring the goods we printed weighing several hundred pounds with as many of my valuable prints,

LEFT: **British soldiers flee Boston by ship. This evacuation marked the end of the siege of Boston.**

BELOW LEFT: **The fledgling U.S. Navy could not compete with the Royal Navy in terms of size, although its ships did well individually—as the USS** *Constitution* **showed against** *Guerrière. Constitution,* **of course, survives to this day, as this photograph of her crew in the rigging attests.**

RIGHT: **Eli Whitney's armory, near New Haven, Connecticut. Armories were a vital development for the American war effort.**

mahogany printing tables, blankets, tearing tubs, broadcloth, sieves, brushes, etc, as I could hurry off with also 3 cows and 2 horses and poultry, such as fowls & ducks plenty, which we shut up in boxes, chests, and by time we got over the river they half died for want of air to breathe in while we were loading a large boat at the wharf, we was obliged to have a person on the top of the chimney to look out the van of the army being at Frankford, I was under the necessity of leaving a great many things behind me."

Young apprentices in various trades were in the thick of the action during the Revolutionary War. Standard apprenticeships were supposed to last seven years. Ben Franklin's autobiography was a favorite of the times, and almost all apprentices knew that revolutionary leaders Franklin and Thomas Paine had left their masters early. In 1779, 15-year-old apprentice Ebenezer Fox wrote:

"I and other boys situated similarly to myself, thought we had wrongs to be redressed; rights to be maintained....We made a direct application of the doctrines we daily heard, in relation to the oppression of our mother country, to our own circumstances....I was doing myself a great injustice by remaining in bondage, when I ought to go free; and that the time was come when I should liberate myself."

Things got even worse for apprentices after the war, however. New laws gave apprentices even less freedom, and a New York law actually doubled the time for runaway apprentices.

But perhaps the greatest application of manufacturing during the Revolutionary War dealt with the establishment of America's first armory. Many felt it would be best for America to manufacture its own arms. In a 1793 letter to the Senate, Henry Knox conceded that weapons manufactured in the United States might be more expensive than those imported from Europe. But, he said, this was of little significance:

"Compared with the solid advantages which would result from extending and perfecting the means upon which our safety may ultimately depend."

The first of these armories, where weapons could be stored and repaired, and ammunition manufactured, was established at an existing site at Springfield, Massachusetts, in 1777. Arms manufacturing was added in 1782, and a permanent facility was established in 1794. The Springfield Armory designed and produced the weapons that armed our forces, including flintlock muskets to percussion rifles, and became the largest manufacturing facility of any kind during the early 1800s. The second armory was established at Harper's Ferry, Virginia. Capacity at these armories increased steadily. By 1811 and 1812, the Springfield Armory produced 20,200 muskets, and the Harper's Ferry Armory produced 22,140.

Federal contracts also gave innovators such as Eli Whitney the capital to begin manufacturing arms. In 1798 Whitney won a contract to manufacture 10,000 muskets. As a way to make up for a shortage of skilled workers, Whitney introduced the process of using interchangeable parts. Thus "machines" replaced artisans and facilitated mass production—which led to what became known as the "American system of manufactures."

GLOSSARY

Apprentice A contractual agreement that binds a person to a craftsman for a specified length of time in return for training in a skill or trade.

Armory A factory where firearms are manufactured and often stored until they are needed by the military.

Bog iron Lumps of iron ore that accumulate in the bottoms of lakes, streams, and peat bogs.

Cash crop An agricultural crop that is grown to sell rather than to feed the growers and their community.

Conestoga wagon A heavy horse-drawn wagon used for transporting goods, primarily in the nineteenth century; named for a town in Pennsylvania.

Cotton gin A machine developed by Eli Whitney that separates the seeds and hulls from the cotton fibers.

Factory A building where goods are manufactured on a large scale.

RIGHT: **The trunk of a longleaf pine tree in Kisatchie National Forest, Louisiana.**

Federalists Early Americans who promoted a strong central government; included leaders such as George Washington and Alexander Hamilton.

Forge A furnace used to heat metal for shaping into useful products.

BELOW: **The first mechanical cotton mill of Samuel Slater in Pawtucket, Rhode Island (tall building in center). Virtually all early American factories relied heavily on water power.**

Founder A person who casts metal, specifically the moveable type used on old printing presses.

Hogshead A barrel, 43 inches high and 26 inches in diameter, used for storing and transporting tobacco and other products.

Indentured servant A person bound by an indenture (contract), usually for four to seven years, in return for transportation to the New World, food, and shelter.

Indigo A tropical plant used as a source of purple dye; once an important cash crop in the South.

Longleaf pine A tall, long-needled pine tree once common in the southeastern U.S., and an important source of shipbuilding lumber and naval stores.

Loom A machine used to weave yarn or thread into cloth.

Loyalist An American colonist who remained loyal to the British during the Revolutionary War.

Manufacture To make a finished product out of raw materials.

Mercantilism An economic theory that promoted expanding a country's power by establishing colonies to provide raw materials and new markets for the home country.

Mill Machinery that grinds grain into flour or meal; also, for some industries such as textile-making, a factory.

Molasses A thick, brown syrup produced from refining sugar; used to make rum.

Naval stores Products such as pitch, tar, and turpentine that come from pine trees and are used in shipbuilding.

Planter A person that owns or manages a plantation.

Rum A distilled alcoholic drink made from molasses.

Shallop A small, open boat powered by oars and sails and used in shallow water.

Shipwright A carpenter who specialized in building ships or making repairs on board a ship.

Smelt To melt metal ore in a fire or furnace to obtain the metal.

Tariff A tax levied by a government on imported or exported goods.

Textile Cloth or fabric that is created on a machine (loom) in a factory.

Tobacco wives Poor women transported from England to the colonies and "sold" as wives to planters, usually for a specified amount of tobacco.

1500

1590 Sir Walter Raleigh declares American fisheries as the "stay and support of the west counties of England."

1600

1607 First permanent English settlement is founded as Jamestown, Virginia, by the Virginia Company and named after King James.

1607 First ship built in the colonies.

1608 First women arrive in Jamestown

1609-10 Starving time in Virginia.

1612 Tobacco is first intentionally cultivated; variety introduced by John Rolfe.

1614 Manhattan Dutch launch their first ship.

1616 More than 2,500 pounds of tobacco exported to England.

1619 First black Africans brought to America; first group of "tobacco wives" arrives in the colonies; first group of "tobacco children" arrives.

1631 First ship built in Massachusetts, *The Blessing of the Bay*, launched.

1632 America's first windmill moved to Copp's Hill in Boston after being built a few years before on a different site.

1633 Boston begins exporting fish.

1639 The first printed press is set up in America, near Cambridge, Massachusetts, by Stephen Daye.

1641 Massachusetts recognizes slavery.

1646 Early iron furnace constructed in Saugus, Virginia.

1651 First documented references to rum (rhum).

1652 Rhode Island recognizes slavery.

1655 John Casor is declared by court as first slave for life in colonies; his owner, Anthony Johnson, is a black freeman.

1661 Virginia recognizes slavery.

1664 Dutch surrender control of New Amsterdam (New York and New Jersey) to British.

1690 First paper money released in colonies; *Publick Occurences* becomes first newspaper (Boston).

1693 Rice is introduced to the Carolina colonies.

ABOVE: **An eagle and American flag grace the stern of the USS *Constitution* at the Charlestown Naval Yard on Boston Harbor.**

1700

1706 Benjamin Franklin born.

1714 Virginia Governor Alexander Spotswood establishes the Germanna settlement.

1715 Christopher Hussey of Nantucket builds a vessel capable of towing sperm whales ashore.

1716 Virginia Governor Alexander Spottswood returns from outing with the "Knights of the Golden Horseshoe."

1726 "Carolina Golde" rice becomes world standard.

1729 Benjamin Franklin buys the *Pennsylvania Gazette*.

1730 Tobacco Inspection acts passed in the colonies.

1733 Molasses Act enacted by Britain to protect British West Indies producers.

1733 Benjamin Franklin produces first *Poor Richard's Almanack*.

1736 Augusta, Georgia, laid out; soon becomes a leading fur-trading center.

1739 Eliza Lucas receives seeds for indigo and other potential crops from her father.

1740 Alexander Spottswood dies.

1744 Fist successful indigo crop raised.

1750 Parliament enacts Iron Act to limit colonial production.

1759 George Washington's first crop of tobacco is deemed unacceptable for sale and export.

1763 French lose French and Indian War.

1763 Printing presses are operational in all 13 colonies.

1764 Sugar Act replaces 1733 Molasses Act.

1768 Samuel Slater born.

1776 Thomas Paine's *Common Sense* published.

1777 Springfield (Massachusetts) Armory established.

1779 Alexander Hamilton advocates for black soldiers.

1783 Massachusetts becomes the first state to abolish slavery.

1785 First Conestoga wagons leave Pennsylvania.

1787 First successful steam vessel, *The Experiment*, was launched on the Delaware River.

1790 Samuel Slater opens first American mill in Pawtucket, Rhode Island.

1790 Benjamin Franklin dies.

1793 Eli Whitney invents cotton gin.

1793 Eliza Lucas dies; George Washington requests to be pallbearer.

1800

1803 President Thomas Jefferson completes Louisiana Purchase from France.

1807 Robert Fulton's steamboat *Clermont* launched.

1814 Boston Manufacturing Company begins production of textiles.

1835 Samuel Slater dies.

ABOVE: **Blackbeard the Pirate was known to place lighted firecrackers in his beard to create a more fearful appearance.**

BOOKS

Adams, James Truslow (ed.), *Album of American History*, New York: Charles Scribner's Sons, 1944.

Allison, Robert J. (ed.), *The Interesting Narrative of the Life of Olaudah Equiano, Written by Himself*, New York: Bedford Books, 1995.

Axelrod, Alan, *The Complete Idiot's Guide to American History*, New York: Alpha Books, 1996.

Bergman, Peter M., *The Chronological History of the Negro in America*, New York: Harper & Row, 1969.

Breen, T.H., *Tobacco Culture, The Mentality of the Great Tidewater Planters on the Eve of Revolution*, Princeton, N.J.: Princeton University Press, 1985.

Carman, Harry J., Harold C. Syrett, Bernard W. Wishy, *A History of the American People, Volume I: To 1877* (Second Edition), New York: Alfred A. Knopf, 1960.

Earle, Alice Morse, *Child Life in Colonial Days*, Stockbridge, Mass.: Berkshire House (reprint edition), 1993.

Fraser, Walter J., *Patriots, Pistols and Petticoats, "Poor Sinful Charles Town" during the American Revolution*, Columbia: University of South Carolina Press, 1993.

Gilmore, Michael T. (ed.), *Early American Literature*, Upper Saddle River, N.J.: Prentice-Hall, 1980.

Hakim, Joy, *Freedom, A History of US*, New York: Oxford University Press, 2003.

Hawke, David Freeman, *Everyday Life in Early America*, New York: Harper & Row, 1988.

Hoose, Phillip, *We Were There, Too! Young People in U.S. History*, New York: Melanie Kroupa Books, 2001.

Isaac, Rhys, *Landon Carter's Uneasy Kingdom: Revolution and Rebellion on a Virginia Plantation*, New York: Oxford University Press, 2004.

Johnston, Robert D., *The Making of America: The History of the United States from 1492 to the Present*, Washington: National Geographic Society, 2002.

Karl, Jean, *America Alive, a History*, New York: Philomel Books, 1994.

King, David C., *Children's Encyclopedia of American History*, New York: DK Publishing, 2003.

Leacock, Elspeth, and Susan Buckley, *Places in Time: A New Atlas of American History*, New York: Houghton Mifflin, 2001.

Leonard Everett, *The Shipbuilders*, Salt Lake City, Utah: Benchmark Books, 1998.

Lester, Julius, *To Be a Slave*, New York: Dial Books, 1998.

Maier, Pauline, Merrit Roe Smith, Alexander Keyssar and Daniel J. Kevles, *A History of the United States: Inventing America, Volume 1: to 1877*, New York: W.W. Norton & Co., 2003.

Mancall, Peter C., *American Encounters; Natives and Newcomers from European Contact to Indian Removal 1500-1850*, Oxford: Routledge, 2000.

McDougall, Walter A., *Freedom Just around the Corner, A New American History*, New York: Harper Collins, 2004.

Meltzer, Milton, *Great Inventions: The Printing Press*, Salt Lake City, Utah: Benchmark Books, 2004.

Morgan, Edmund S., *The Genuine Article; A Historian Looks at Early America*, New York: W.W. Norton & Co., 2004.

Neill, Peter (ed.), *American Sea Writing; A Literary Anthology*, New York: Library of America, 2000.

Raphael, Ray, *A People's History of the American Revolution*, New York: The New Press, 2001.

Rich, E. E., *The Hudson's Bay Company 1670-1870*, New York: The MacMillan Company, 1958.

Russell, Carl P., *Guns on the Early Frontier*, Berkeley: University of California Press, 1957.

Schlesinger, Arthur M. Sr., Dixon Ryan Fox, and Mark C. Carnes, *A History of American Life*, New York: Simon & Schuster (revised edition), 1996.

Stiles, T.J., *In Their Own Words: The Colonizers, Early European Settlers and the Shaping of North America*, New York: Perigee, 1998.

Taylor, Dale, *The Writer's Guide to Everyday Life in Colonial America, from 1607-1783*, Cincinnati: Writer's Digest, 1997.

Tunis, Edwin, *Colonial Living*, Baltimore: Johns Hopkins University Press (reprint edition), 1999.

Virga, Vincent, *Eyes of the Nation, a Visual History of the United States*, New York: Alfred A. Knopf, 1977.

Wilkinson, Philip, and Michael Pollard, *The Industrial Revolution*, Langhorne, Pa.: Chelsea House Publishers, 1995.

Wilmore, Kathy, *A Day in the Life of a Colonial Printer*, New York: Powerkids Press, 2000.

Wood, Betty, *The Origins of American Slavery*, New York: Hill & Wang, 1997.

Wroth, Lawrence C., *The Colonial Printer*, Mineola, N.Y.: Dover Publications, 1994.

Zinn, Howard, *A People's History of the United States: 1492–Present*, New York: Harper Collins, 1999.

WEB SITES

"American History from Discovery to the Colonial Period"
http://schools.bcsd.com/garza/library/links2/ss1.htm

"The American Printing History Association"
http://www.printinghistory.org/htm/journal/contents.html

"Breed's Collection of Tobacco History Sites"
http://smokingsides.com/docs/hist.html

"Collected State of the Union Addresses of U.S. Presidents"
http://www.infoplease.com/t/hist/state-of-the-union/13.html

"Colonial American Digital Library"
http://www.academicinfo.net/usearlylibrary.html

"Documenting the American South"
http://docsouth.unc.edu/index.html

"The Economies of the 1720s"
http://www2.sjsu.edu/faculty/watkins/colonies1720.htm

"The Founders' Constitution"
http://press-pubs.uchicago.edu/founders

"Historical Society of Pennsylvania"
http://www.hsp.org

"Nicotine Is a Drug!"
http://www.cigarettesmokingkills.com/Timeline.html

"The Online Library of Liberty: George Washington (1732-1799)"
http://oll.libertyfund.org/Intros/Washington.php

"Slavery in the North"
http://www.slavenorth.com/

"Tobacco: The Early History of a New World Crop"
http://www.nps.gov/colo/Jthanout/TobaccoHistory.html

"U.S. History Outlines and Charts"
http://www.polytechnic.org/faculty/gfeldmeth/lecturesok.html

"Virtual American Biographies"
http://www.famousamericans.net

SET INDEX

Page numbers in italic indicate illustrations or maps. Those in bold indicate volume numbers.

Index by Marian Anderson